$7.95
2.95 pb.

ARMS ACROSS THE SEA

Philip J. Farley
Stephen S. Kaplan
William H. Lewis

ARMS ACROSS THE SEA

The Brookings Institution
Washington, D.C.

Copyright © 1978 by
THE BROOKINGS INSTITUTION
1775 Massachusetts Avenue, N.W., Washington, D.C. 20036

Library of Congress Cataloging in Publication Data:
Farley, Philip, 1916–
  Arms across the sea.
  Includes bibliographical references and index.
    1. Munitions—United States.   2. Military assis-
tance, American. · I. Kaplan, Stephen S., joint author.
II. Lewis, William Hubert, 1928– joint author.
III. Title.
HD9743.U6F37   382'.45'62340973   77-91804
ISBN 0-8157-2746-1
ISBN 0-8157-2745-3 pbk.

9 8 7 6 5 4 3 2 1

THE BROOKINGS INSTITUTION is an independent organization devoted to nonpartisan research, education, and publication in economics, government, foreign policy, and the social sciences generally. Its principal purposes are to aid in the development of sound public policies and to promote public understanding of issues of national importance.

The Institution was founded on December 8, 1927, to merge the activities of the Institute for Government Research, founded in 1916, the Institute of Economics, founded in 1922, and the Robert Brookings Graduate School of Economics and Government, founded in 1924.

The Board of Trustees is responsible for the general administration of the Institution, while the immediate direction of the policies, program, and staff is vested in the President, assisted by an advisory committee of the officers and staff. The by-laws of the Institution state: "It is the function of the Trustees to make possible the conduct of scientific research, and publication, under the most favorable conditions, and to safeguard the independence of the research staff in the pursuit of their studies and in the publication of the results of such studies. It is not a part of their function to determine, control, or influence the conduct of particular investigations or the conclusions reached."

The President bears final responsibility for the decision to publish a manuscript as a Brookings book. In reaching his judgment on the competence, accuracy, and objectivity of each study, the President is advised by the director of the appropriate research program and weighs the views of a panel of expert outside readers who report to him in confidence on the quality of the work. Publication of a work signifies that it is deemed a competent treatment worthy of public consideration but does not imply endorsement of conclusions or recommendations.

The Institution maintains its position of neutrality on issues of public policy in order to safeguard the intellectual freedom of the staff. Hence interpretations or conclusions in Brookings publications should be understood to be solely those of the authors and should not be attributed to the Institution, to its trustees, officers, or other staff members, or to the organizations that support its research.

Foreword

Since the Second World War the United States has become the world's largest exporter of arms. During the past decade, the United States agreed to transfer weapons and supplementary equipment and to render related services with an aggregate value of over $100 billion in 1977 dollars to a large number of foreign nations. Americans have also trained foreign military personnel, exported technology for the foreign production of U.S.-designed armaments, given economic aid to support defense efforts by other countries, and lent ships abroad.

Controversy over transfers of military goods and services led to legal restrictions enacted by Congress and in 1976 to the passage of the omnibus International Security Assistance and Arms Export Control Act. President Jimmy Carter, in a statement shortly after he took office in 1977, advocated still greater restrictions on U.S. arms transfers abroad.

How does the export of arms affect the interests and values of the United States? What benefits do these transfers have? What risks do they entail? To what extent and to whom should the United States export war materiel? The authors of this book explore the role of the United States in the world arms market, the development of U.S. military aid and sales programs, the question of coproduction, and the kinds of choices policymakers face in offering to export armaments and in responding to requests for them from foreign nations. They suggest criteria for evaluating the utility of military transfers and conclude that U.S. interests might be best served by practicing restraint in the export of arms and other military equipment.

Philip J. Farley, a former Brookings senior fellow, is Deputy U.S. Special Representative for Nonproliferation Matters in the Department of State. Stephen S. Kaplan is a research associate in the Brookings Foreign Policy Studies program. William H. Lewis was a senior fellow at Brookings in 1974–75 while on leave from the Department of State.

The Institution and the authors are grateful to the Rockefeller Foundation for financial support that helped make this study possible. The authors also thank their Brookings colleagues Henry Owen and Joseph A. Yager for counsel in this project; Paul C. Kinsinger, who provided research assistance; Alice M. Carroll, who edited the manuscript; Penelope S. Harpold, who verified the factual content of the study; and Jeanane Patterson and others, who typed its various drafts. The index was prepared by Florence Robinson.

The views expressed in this book are the authors' alone and should not be ascribed to the Rockefeller Foundation or to the officers, trustees, or other staff members of the Brookings Institution.

BRUCE K. MAC LAURY
President

March 1978
Washington, D.C.

Contents

Text Tables

CHAPTER ONE

The United States and the World Arms Market

The transfer of arms by the United States to foreign countries has been a troublesome issue. During the past decade the public argument over military assistance and arms sales developed into a sharp contest between Congress and the executive branch over the shaping of U.S. arms transfer policy. The crucial points of conflict have been the place of arms and military power in U.S. foreign policy, the purposes for which U.S. arms should be provided, and the role of Congress in regard to both broad policies and major program decisions. The debate has extended to the question of the U.S. role in the world, in regional conflicts, and in maintaining military balances. A major policy change announced early in the Carter administration did not end this discussion.

Debate over U.S. Arms Transfers

The original premise of the integrated program of security assistance that developed after World War II was to protect the United States and its allies against a unified and expansionist international Communist movement. The tragic consequences of U.S. isolationism had convinced Americans that aggression should not be permitted to succeed. Threats after the war to Greece and Turkey, elsewhere in Europe, and then to South Korea were clear challenges. As the leading proponent of collective security and international organization, the United States looked to the United Nations to respond; where the United Nations could not act, the United States created new regional organizations for the purpose.

1

As a last resort it was prepared to intervene unilaterally to protect its worldwide interests and American beliefs and values.

The cold war and containment premises on which the security assistance and foreign military sales programs operated no longer adequately apply to the international scene. The split between the Soviet Union and China has been the most conspicuous sign of a more complex world, but even militant Communist states such as North Korea, North Vietnam, Cuba, and Cambodia have nationalist and self-determined governments pursuing their own interests. Although they may receive support from the Soviet Union or China, they are not tools of their powerful backers. However brutal or unattractive, their regimes represent forces of local, or at most regional, influence rather than orchestrated parts of a unified global threat.

The United States in the 1970s abandoned the notion of a bipolar struggle between free and Communist blocs and asserted a policy that stressed complexity and instability in the world and focused on building a structure of order to support peace, economic cooperation, and growth. Secretary of State Henry Kissinger in his policy statements stressed international security problems, relations among major military and industrial powers, U.S. world leadership, and U.S. military power. Often, however, the United States treated international and national security problems as a struggle for resources, power, markets, and influence, where U.S. political, commercial, and other interests were to be advanced. Thus security assistance and arms sales remained major tools of U.S. foreign policy, to be used as general rather than ad hoc instruments with which to grapple with security problems. The idea of rivalry between Marxist and free societies and of the United States as leader and major support of the latter camp continued.

This emphasis on military power as a primary tool of foreign policy called for large-scale grants of military assistance, substantial government concessionary and cost-of-money credit for arms sales, an integrated global arms-transfer program affording presidential initiative and flexibility within congressional policy guidelines, an active government role in consummating cash arms sales to rich nations, and use of both security assistance and arms sales as means of political influence in the developing world. It required a large measure of decision-making authority and freedom of action for the executive branch.

Within Congress a countervailing effort was made to bring the foreign aid and arms sales programs under closer surveillance and control. Congressional leaders emphasized the U.S. role of active and constructive partner rather than world leader, with a stress on economic and other nonmilitary activities, cooperation, and development assistance rather than military power and aid. They called for phasing out security assistance, with ad hoc exceptions, and for restraint in arms sales. In short, they advocated a policy of moderation in arms transfers.

Immediately after President Jimmy Carter's inauguration, the new administration carried out a review of U.S. arms transfer policy.[1] On the basis of this study the President issued a statement of his policy:

> I have concluded that the United States will henceforth view arms transfers as an exceptional foreign policy implement, to be used only in instances where it can be clearly demonstrated that the transfer contributes to our national security interests. We will continue to utilize arms transfers to promote our security and the security of our close friends. But in the future the burden of persuasion will be on those who favor a particular arms sale, rather than those who oppose it.[2]

The President proposed specific measures restricting and tightening control of the sale of U.S. weapons abroad. He further related that human rights considerations would be weighed in the formulation of security assistance programs and that the economic impact of arms transfers on the economies of less developed nations receiving U.S. economic assistance would be assessed.

To many observers this statement indicated an intent to limit the flow of arms from the United States abroad to an even greater degree than Congress had urged. While the Nixon and Ford administrations were favorably disposed to using arms transfers as an instrument of U.S. policy, and Congress had passed legislation requiring a cautious case-by-case examination, President Carter proposed that arms transfers be used only as an "exceptional foreign policy implement" and presented a blanketlike approach. President Carter did exclude from application of his policy nations with which the United States has a major defense treaty, and he reconfirmed "our historic responsibilities to assure the security of the state of Israel." The policy was also initiated, he said, "in the full understanding that actual reductions in the worldwide traffic in arms will require multilateral cooperation."[3]

1. See *Arms Transfer Policy, Report to Congress* (GPO, 1977).
2. "Conventional Arms Transfer Policy: Statement by the President, May 19, 1977," *Weekly Compilation of Presidential Documents*, vol. 13 (May 23, 1977), pp. 756–57.
3. Ibid.

Any approach to U.S. arms transfer policy must be considered not only in terms of United States interests and bilateral relations but the wider fabric of international political, economic, and security relationships. It is misleading to view the world that has succeeded the bipolar world of cold war as one organized around three nations (the United States, the USSR, and China), five (adding Europe and Japan), or some other small number of powers. More basic to understanding the evolving international situation is acceptance of the emotional and political force of nationalism. Nationalism has proved to be stubbornly resistant to ideological pressure or economic leverage. It cannot be blinked in any realistic appraisal of the arms trade, the prospect for arms control, or the prevalence of conflict. In a world of independent sovereign states, many political and social systems—military regimes or socialist societies—will be unattractive to Americans. Their violent or revolutionary birth and their methods of establishing authority in the face of intractable economic problems, sharp social or other divisions, and a fuzzy but powerful sense of national identity may upset Americans. Yet for such states the determination to find their own way may be the strongest force against outside interference or domination by U.S. rivals or opponents. If France, Turkey, Ecuador, and the Philippines have at times been difficult allies for the United States, so have Indonesia, Rumania, Cuba, Egypt, and even North Vietnam and North Korea for the Communist powers. Resistance to Soviet or Chinese dominance neither begins with nor depends solely on the United States.

The process of decolonization and of defining and establishing new states has all but ended with the collapse of the Portuguese empire. This and the demise of the cold war signal the close of the postwar transitional period. With China in the United Nations and the Security Council, oil power a virtually accepted fact, and the divided states that have been major flashpoints coming to a modus vivendi (consolidation for the two Vietnams, recognition and UN admission for the two Germanies), the outlines of the world structure of at least the next decade have emerged.

Within the new structure lie many long-standing or incipient conflicts: the Arab-Israeli standoff, the Sino-Soviet dispute and contest for influence, the North-South hostility in Korea. The new nations are seeking a more prominent role internationally; the principle of self-determination has still to be worked out in many of them. Colonial vestiges remain in the white minority-ruled states of South Africa and Rhodesia. Disputed boundaries are still to be settled in many parts of the world. Submerged peoples, such as the Palestinians and Kurds, continue to have grievances. Territorial, social, tribal, religious, and other differences will erupt in wars and insurgencies.

When do U.S. interests call for either military assistance, arms sales, or the transfer of technology that would allow other countries to produce weapons? Discrimination in finding answers to this question is required not just to avoid being involved, but because these instruments of policy do not always serve to contain conflict and to establish a viable local balance of forces.

A major aim of the security assistance program should be to keep to a bare minimum the number of countries included and the amount of aid given. The goal ideally would be to phase the program out. Coinciding interests, not aid, form the basis for rewarding and mutually pleasing relationships. Security assistance tends to increase dependence and to force on the United States responsibilities greater than its interests. Self-reliance by allies and friends allows the United States to resist embroilment where it prefers to do so. Security assistance should be given for specific and explicit purposes and without the connotation of being a permanent subsidy. The United States should prefer sales to aid and, as an intermediate step, credits to grants, in order to place U.S. relationships on a firmer footing and allow greater U.S. freedom of action. If only for this reason, the United States should support the economic development of security assistance recipients. As a means to gain or retain influence with a foreign regime, security assistance should be used cautiously.

Sales will be useful to support U.S. interests insofar as they serve to deter mutual antagonists or help stabilize situations where conflict harmful to U.S. interests might otherwise occur. Sales that would create imbalance and increase the likelihood of instability should be avoided. Sales should not be made for economic reasons. Although the dollar return is good for the U.S. economy and important to particular corporations and communities, economic promotion risks strongly the perversion of larger U.S. interests, including long-term economic ones. Sales too can increase dependence, particularly of nations that do not have an adequate number of trained personnel to operate and maintain equipment. The United States wants to avoid the dilemma of having to allow U.S. military and civilian personnel to aid the military activities of a purchasing nation or suffering a sharp decline in relations with that nation and perhaps consigning it to military defeat. For this reason, the United States should not seek exclusivity in sales. Sales by other nations can allow the United States greater freedom of action when a crisis develops; economic returns that support the defense industry of European allies are also of value to long-term U.S. security interests. Thus restraint in arms sales is a valid policy even if it means a partial loss of sales to European competitors.

The transfer of arms production technology offers little gain for the United States and should be limited. Direct sales are preferable to foreign assembly, and the latter is more desirable than licensed or joint production. Coproduction may be preferable to another country's decision to establish an advanced arms industry, however. Here security and economic interests are in closer agreement. When it is sensible to allow coproduction, explicit agreements should be made covering production for export to third countries. These agreements should provide for the security protection of arms and their technology, retransfers, and the uses to which those arms may be put as well as list grounds for terminating deliveries or the supply of spare parts if arms are used for unacceptable purposes.

Decisions on security assistance, arms sales, and export of military technology should be taken with great deliberation, after exposure to an adversary process, on a case-by-case basis. Long-standing interests and objectives will not be served best by across-the-board policies, but rather by recognition that there is no substitute for an understanding of U.S. interests, careful judgment, and willingness to be selective.

The World Arms Market

Most independent nations have some kind of armed forces to insure internal order, territorial integrity, and national dignity. Whether new or old, superpower or ministate, few nations judge themselves able to maintain only a constabulary rather than a military establishment.[4] In 1975 the military expenditures of 142 countries amounted to approximately $371 billion, or 6 percent of their aggregate gross national product.[5] Twenty-eight developed countries spent $290 billion of the total; slightly

4. In 1975, 142 countries either had a military establishment or were purchasing military equipment; see U.S. Arms Control and Disarmament Agency (ACDA), *World Military Expenditures and Arms Transfers, 1966–1975* (GPO, 1976), table 2.

5. Ibid., p. 14. Detailed data are not available on expenditures after 1975.

less than 6 percent of their GNP went to military budgets, in contrast to 7.2 percent a decade earlier. World military expenditures had totaled $160 billion in 1965 and had grown rapidly until 1968, when they began to level off in real terms: over the decade the aggregate military budgets of the developed countries grew at a rate of 2 percent annually; the rate for the developing countries, however, was more than 6 percent (individual developing nations spent anywhere from less than 1 percent to more than 35 percent of their GNP for military purposes.[6]

Arms Imports

Most countries have no arms industry, or at best a rudimentary one, and must acquire military equipment from other, more industrialized nations on a cash, credit, or grant basis. In 1975 the world arms trade—deliveries of arms by nations to one another—amounted to over $9.7 billion, or about 2.5 percent of the $371 billion in military expenditures. Almost three-quarters of these arms were purchased by developing countries (see table 1-1), and they constituted the great bulk of these countries' new equipment, which absorbed 9 percent of their military budgets. Only a small number of these countries manufactured or assembled a significant part of their arms and equipment—for example, China, India, and Israel.

In many developed countries, military expenditures leveled off in recent years as a result of changing views of the NATO-Warsaw Pact military balance in Europe and because of the influence of détente. In developing countries, expenditures and imports have risen with an increase in the number of national military establishments and in national wealth. The pattern is not uniform, however; there are temporary peaks in the share of resources going to particular areas at times of conflict (Nigeria, India-Pakistan) and prolonged ones for regions where there is protracted confrontation and tension (Middle East, North-South Korea, Indochina) or a sharp increase in disposable resources (Persian Gulf). Most U.S. arms transfers in recent years have gone to the Middle East and to industrialized allies in Europe.

Rising values of arms imports in part reflect worldwide inflation and the higher unit costs of sophisticated late-model military equipment. In the Middle East they are due to major orders from Israel to the United States and from Egypt and Syria to the Soviet Union for reequipment

6. Calculated from ibid., tables 1 and 2; and ACDA, *World Military Expenditures and Arms Transfers, 1965–1974* (GPO, 1975), tables 1 and 2.

Table 1-1. *Imports of Arms by Developed and Developing Nations,*
1966–75
Billions of current dollars

Time period	Developed nations	Developing nations	Total
1966–70	8.5	18.2	26.7
1971	1.7	4.7	6.4
1972	2.1	6.6	8.7
1973	1.5	8.1	9.6
1974	2.6	6.7	9.3
1975	2.6	7.1	9.7
1971–75	10.5	33.2	43.7
1966–75	19.0	51.4	70.4

Source: Calculated from U.S. Arms Control and Disarmament Agency (ACDA), *World Military Expenditures and Arms Transfers, 1966–1975* (GPO, 1976), p. 56.

and for modernization after the massive losses of equipment during the October 1973 war. The parties to the Arab-Israeli conflict are now heavily armed with new weapons, although Egypt's inventories have begun to deteriorate as a result of Cairo's poor relations with Moscow and Soviet unwillingness to supply spare parts and the support necessary to maintain equipment it supplied earlier.

The rise in oil income has also stimulated arms purchases by the Persian Gulf states. In these nations, and also in Libya and Algeria, there is no prospect of major hostilities that would use up equipment—beyond their taking active roles in a fifth Arab-Israeli war. These countries have the money to buy what they want. Their arms imports will be determined, first, by their perception of what they need and, second, by what they can absorb. All of these states are in early—though different—stages of development; their levels of literacy are low, their societies and governments traditional, and their needs multiple. They are only beginning to feel the impact of recent wealth and the prospect of a new way of life.

Iran, Saudi Arabia, and Kuwait have begun equipping and training their forces with a full range of sophisticated equipment, giving priority to arms and military establishments. It will take a number of years, however, for the equipment on order from the United States to be delivered. And absorbing the arms will place unanticipated demands on skilled manpower and the national infrastructure, causing conflicts in priority with other areas of the economy.

Britain and France, like the United States, makes substantial sales of arms in the Persian Gulf area, and the Soviet Union is the principal supplier of Iraq and Syria. The actual flow of arms to the area clearly will be rising in the next few years.

In other areas, there have been no recent spurts in imports, and in the future there will be counterpressures against major increases in the arms trade. Some modernization should continue in NATO countries in response to Soviet modernization and U.S. calls for burden-sharing within the alliance, but tight domestic budgets and the economic effects of inflation and foreign-exchange stringencies will limit acquisitions and shift emphasis to national or joint production efforts in Europe. Inflation and a shortage of foreign exchange should also work to hold down arms imports in the developing countries that are not oil producers unless there are conflicts such as the Indo-Pakistani clashes or the Nigerian civil war.

The impact of higher costs of food, oil, and fertilizer cannot yet be measured in the arms purchases of many developing and developed countries. Arms expenditures often have a privileged place in national budgets and import decisions, reflecting powerful national drives to attain security, prestige, and self-pride (see table 1-2). For example, despite a low per capita income and hundreds of millions of people living at the subsistence level, India and China have been able to plan and fund modern military establishments and support nuclear programs. The United States in 1975 had been repaid on schedule all but $4.9 *million* of a total of over $16 *billion* in military credit it had extended since 1950.[7] This priority claim on disposable capital and foreign exchange is extremely costly to developing countries. Their imports of commodities and manufactured goods in 1975 totaled $242.4 billion, and arms imports represented 3 percent of the total.[8] Except in fortunate countries with oil or export surpluses or in unfortunate countries with overriding security problems and military needs, arms imports are likely to be closely questioned, though they will be blocked only sometimes.

Policies of the Arms Suppliers

Nine suppliers were the source of 97 percent of world arms imports during the period 1966–75 (see table 1-3). The United States not only

7. Secretary of Defense James R. Schlesinger, "Annual Defense Department Report, FY 1976 and FY 197T" (Feb. 5, 1975; processed), pt. 4, p. 30.

8. International Monetary Fund, *International Financial Statistics*, vol. 30 (February 1977), p. 33. Arms imports are from ACDA, *World Military Expenditures and Arms Transfers, 1966–1975*, p. 56.

Table 1-2. *Percentage of Gross National Product Allocated for Military Expenditures as Related to Per-Capita GNP, Selected Countries, 1975*

GNP per capita	Countries where share of GNP allocated to military is				
	More than 10 percent	*5–10 percent*	*2–4.9 percent*	*1–1.9 percent*	*Less than 1 percent*
Less than $100	Cambodia, North Vietnam	Chad, Laos, Somalia	Burundi, Ethiopia, Mali, Rwanda, Upper Volta	Afghanistan	...
$100–199	South Vietnam	Pakistan, Yemen (Sana)	Burma, Central African Republic, Guinea, India, Indonesia, Tanzania, Zaire	Benin, Haiti	Bangladesh, Gambia, Lesotho, Malawi, Nepal, Niger, Sierra Leone
$200–299	Egypt, People's Republic of China	Yemen (Aden)	Equatorial Guinea, Mauritania, Sudan, Uganda	Cameroon, Honduras, Kenya, Madagascar, Togo	Sri Lanka
$300–499	Jordan, North Korea	Albania, South Korea	Bolivia, Congo, Morocco, Nigeria, Philippines, Rhodesia, Thailand	Colombia, El Salvador, Ghana, Senegal	Botswana, Liberia, Mozambique, Swaziland

$500–999	Syria	Cuba, Malaysia, Mongolia, Republic of China	Algeria, Angola, Brazil, Chile, Guyana, Nicaragua, Peru, Turkey, Uruguay, Zambia	Dominican Republic, Ecuador, Guatemala, Ivory Coast, Paraguay, Tunisia	Costa Rica, Fiji, Mauritius, Mexico, Panama
$1,000–1,999	Iran, Iraq	Bulgaria, Portugal, Rumania	Argentina, Cyprus, Lebanon, South Africa, Yugoslavia	...	Barbados, Jamaica, Malta, Surinam
$2,000–2,999	Israel, Oman	Greece, Hungary, Poland, Singapore	Bahrain, Italy, Spain, Venezuela	Gabon, Ireland	Trinidad and Tobago
More than $3,000	Soviet Union	Czechoslovakia, East Germany, Qatar, Saudi Arabia, United States	Australia, Belgium, Canada, Denmark, France, West Germany, Kuwait, Netherlands, Norway, Sweden, United Kingdom	Austria, Finland, Libya, Luxembourg, New Zealand, Switzerland	Iceland, Japan, United Arab Emirates

Source: ACDA, *World Military Expenditures and Arms Transfers, 1966–1975*, p. 6.

sold the largest amount ($34.9 billion, half the world total of $70.4 billion), but also served the most customers—eighty-one.[9] France and the United Kingdom, major trading nations that promote arms sales for commercial reasons, sold to 73 and 61 countries, respectively. The Soviet Union shipped to 44 and China to 16 (North Vietnam, North Korea, and Pakistan received almost 91 percent of the Chinese exports).

Some of the principal suppliers—Canada, West Germany, and Sweden—follow an explicit policy of not selling arms in regions of tension or conflict, partly to stay out of trouble and partly to try to moderate conflicts rather than to feed them. As a result Canada and West Germany sell mainly to allies. Japan, the world's third-ranking industrial nation, could be a major manufacturer and exporter of arms, but its military policy has long been limited to self-defense. Japan does not export arms to active or potential parties to an international dispute (or to Communist countries or countries embargoed by the United Nations). Its arms exports are predominantly nonlethal items such as support vessels, transport aircraft or helicopters, and electronic gear; they averaged less than $10 million annually in value during the period 1966–75, a modest figure compared with over $100 million annually for Canada and West Germany and over $20 million for much smaller Sweden.[10]

The arms transfer policies of the Soviet Union, China, and the United States are dominated by political and security considerations. The United States, because it is a major trading nation with commercial ties to most other nations, has in the past taken into account American economic and commercial interests—especially when adverse balance-of-payments and balance-of-trade factors have come into play, as they have in the 1970s—in prospective sales to industrial or oil-rich states. But political and security factors control U.S. sales decisions.

In the United States the government dominates the arms business. Arms manufacturers have at times engaged in aggressive advertising and sales tactics, but the pre-World War II image of private "merchants of death" setting the pace of the arms race does not fit the current reality.

9. A number of other countries made commercial purchases none of which exceeded $250,000 each during this period. U.S. Department of Defense, Defense Security Assistance Agency, "Fiscal Year Series" (DSAA, Apr. 15, 1975; processed).

10. ACDA, *World Military Expenditures and Arms Transfers, 1966–1975,* table 2.

Table 1-3. *Shares of Principal Suppliers in World Arms Market, 1966–75*
Millions of current dollars

Supplier	1966–70	1971	1972	1973	1974	1975	1966–75
United States	13,430	3,380	4,100	5,020	4,160	4,850	34,940
Soviet Union	7,770	1,610	2,420	2,860	2,870	2,610	20,140
France	896	154	534	564	561	504	3,213
United Kingdom	683	178	312	333	463	378	2,347
People's Republic of China	832	251	396	232	321	191	2,223
West Germany	514	130	226	26	223	257	1,376
Czechoslovakia	667	122	121	106	76	118	1,210
Canada	605	187	153	74	109	73	1,201
Poland	742	173	91	61	20	41	1,128
Others	592	174	344	290	484	703	2,587
Total	26,731	6,359	8,697	9,566	9,287	9,725	70,365

Source: Calculated from ACDA, *World Military Expenditures and Arms Transfers, 1966–1975,* table 4.

Commercial sales of arms and related technical data require a government license and are the smaller part of arms sales.

U.S. Agreements to Transfer Arms

Overall since 1946, grant military aid has outstripped U.S. government sales of arms—$69 billion versus about $53 billion through fiscal 1976 (table 1-4).[11] Government sales have been much greater than commercial sales. In fiscal 1950–76 (information is unavailable for earlier years) commercial arms deliveries totaled $6 billion. Most of the commercial deliveries—$5 billion in value—were made in fiscal 1966–76, when deliveries on governmental sales orders totaled $20 billion.[12]

In the 1970s U.S. government sales began to exceed grant aid both in the value of sales agreements arrived at and in actual exports of arms.[13] Government sales began to rise in the mid-1960s when an adverse balance of payments and criticism of the financial burden of U.S. troop de-

11. Grant military aid includes what is listed in table 1-4 as security assistance minus security supporting assistance and foreign military sales credits.
12. DSAA, *Foreign Military Sales and Military Assistance Facts, November 1975* (DSAA, 1976), pp. 14, 16, and 22, and *December 1976* (1977), pp. 12, 14, and 16; DSAA, "Security Assistance Program, Vol. 1, FY 1978," Congressional Presentation (DSAA, 1977; processed), p. 23.
13. The reversal began even earlier in transfers to nations not engaged in the Vietnam War.

Table 1-4. U.S. Security Assistance and Arms Sales, Fiscal 1946–78

Billions of current dollars

Program	1946–65	1966–70	1971–75	1946–75	1976	197T[a]	1977, estimated	1978, proposed
Security assistance								
Military assistance grants[b]	31.5	3.3	3.3	38.1	0.2	0.1	0.4	0.3
Military assistance grants, service funded[c]	0.2	7.0	11.7	18.8	d	d	n.a.	n.a.
Transfers from excess stocks[e]	2.8	2.2	1.6	6.6	0.1	*	0.1	*
Security supporting assistance[f]	11.6	3.2	3.7	18.5	1.1	0.9	1.8	1.9
Foreign military sales credits[g]	0.6	1.3	4.0	5.8	2.2	0.6	2.0	2.2
Other grants[h]	1.6	0.1	2.5	4.3	0.8	0.1	n.a.	n.a.
Total	48.2	17.1	26.8	92.1	4.4	1.6	4.2	4.4
Government sales orders[i]	8.5	5.9	29.6	44.0	8.7	0.8	8.8	7.7
Commercial deliveries[j]	1.1	1.4	2.3	4.8	1.2	0.3	1.2	1.2

Sources: U.S. Agency for International Development, U.S. Overseas Loans and Grants and Assistance from International Organizations: Obligations and Loan Authorizations, July 1, 1945–June 30, 1975 (AID, 1976), pp. 1–3 and 6, and July 1, 1945–September 30, 1976 (1977), pp. 1–3 and 6; U.S. Department of Defense, Defense Security Assistance Agency, Foreign Military Sales and Military Assistance Facts, November, 1975 (DSAA, 1976), pp. 14–22, and December 1976 (1977), p. 16; and DSAA, "Security Assistance Program, 1976 and 197T," Congressional Presentation (DSAA, 1975; processed), "Fiscal Year 1977" (1976), and "Volume 1, FY 1978." Figures are rounded.

n.a. = not available.

* less than $50 million.

a. Transitional budget, July 1–Sept. 30, 1976, when the beginning of the fiscal year was moved from July 1 to October 1.

b. Includes funds for international military education and training program. Grants drop after 1966 because much of the Southeast Asian burden is transferred to the military assistance, service funded program.

c. Funds provided through Department of Defense budget to South Korea, Laos, the Philippines, Thailand, and South Vietnam.

d. AID, Obligations and Loan Authorizations, July 1, 1945–September 30, 1976, lists $239 million in fiscal 1976 and $38 million in fiscal 197T as obligated to this program. These figures are not included in DSAA, "Security Assistance Program, Volume 1, FY 1978."

e. Figures reflect full value of articles at acquisition.

f. Initiated in 1953 under the Mutual Security Act.

g. Initiated in 1955.

h. Includes the military portions of Greek-Turkish aid, naval aid to the Republic of China, aid to the Philippines under Public Law 454, transfers of materiel to South Korea under P.L. 91-652, and vessel loans (which are treated as grants because of their long duration).

i. May or may not include foreign military sales credits (listed above) in any given year. Data are from 1950 onward.

j. Data only available from 1960 onward. Data cover only actual exports of arms by private contractors; no data on commercial sales orders are available.

ployments overseas and military aid led to an emphasis on sales to wealthy allies (Western Europe, especially Germany, and Japan and Australia) as an offsetting measure. The conviction that arms sales provide important political influence and a way to knit relations with Persian Gulf states as well as recoup oil dollars reinforced government interest in arms sales; witness the notable rise in sales to the Middle East in the 1970s (table 1-5).

In fiscal 1974 U.S. sales orders jumped to $10.6 billion (from $5.8 billion in fiscal 1973), while grant military aid totaled only $3.7 billion (declining from $5.2 billion in fiscal 1973). By fiscal 1976 grant military aid equaled only $1.1 billion; foreign military sales in that year amounted to $8.9 billion. The amount of sales agreed to grew so rapidly that in 1977 the backlog in deliveries was estimated at $32 billion, and deliveries in fiscal 1977–80 were expected to reach $26 billion (in 1975 dollars), even assuming a 40 percent reduction in new agreements during that time.[14]

An important element in the growth of government sales has been the use of foreign military sales credits; they totaled $8 billion through fiscal 1976. Between fiscal 1971 and 1975, credits equaled about 13 percent of government sales; this figure jumped to 25 percent in fiscal 1976 and appears to be remaining there. Thus government funds continue to play an important role in U.S. transfers of arms, even though client states can no longer look confidently toward receiving military assistance from the United States.

14. *Arms Transfer Policy*, pp. 55 and 58.

Table 1-5. *Regional Distribution of U.S. Security Assistance^a and Governme*
Millions of current dollars

Region	1946–65 Assistance	Sales	1966–70 Assistance	Sales	1971–75 Assistance	Sales
Europe	20,949	4,185	1,522	3,221	1,712	6,80:
NATO[d]	12,697	4,019	77	2,884	38	5,07(
Greece	2,175	2	459	64	446	91
Turkey	3,577	1	870	6	982	30(
Yugoslavia	1,154	11	0	1	0	:
Other[e]	1,346	152	116	266	246	50.
Middle East	1,427	2,332	1,166	1,512	5,122	19,36(
Saudi Arabia	90	2,140	192	112	15	4,97:
Israel	40	67	237	516	4,410	4,31(
Iran	1,003	70	606	775	16	9,52:
Other[g]	294	55	131	109	681	55.
South Asia	1,493	89	29	54	5	10(
India	137	54	7	6	0	1
Pakistan	1,321	35	12	48	1	9:
Other[h]	35	0	10	0	4	(
East Asia	17,769	156	12,149	300	16,153	1,32
South Vietnam	3,611	0	7,828	0	11,069	
Cambodia and Laos[i]	2,600	9	721	0	1,573	(
Thailand	854	1	566	25	414	5
Taiwan	3,789	3	759	138	594	56
South Korea	4,765	0	2,026	5	2,120	34.
Japan	1,238	136	2	120	0	19:
Philippines	718	5	137	2	204	3:
Other[j]	194	2	110	10	179	12(
Latin America	1,534	257	541	148	588	63:
Brazil	405	43	106	45	169	16.
Other South America	862	191	243	99	338	44:
Central American and Caribbean republics	267	23	192	4	81	3
Africa	554	9	269	55	247	39.
Ethiopia	111	1	71	0	100	3.
Morocco	113	0	43	27	61	31(
Zaire	215	0	68	2	30	2(
Other[k]	115	8	87	26	56	2:
Other nations	133	1,339	5	578	3	78.
Australia	118	596	5	277	0	39.
New Zealand	2	38	0	62	3	2.
Canada	13	705	0	179	0	36(
Total[l]	43,859	8,367	15,681	5,808	23,830	29,41

Table notes are on page 18.

les^b of Arms, Fiscal 1946–78

	1946–75		1976		197T^c		1977, estimated		1978, proposed	
	ssistance	Sales	Assistance	Sales	Assistance	Sales	Assistance	Sales	Assistance	Sales
	24,183	14,208	205	1,089	249	128	637	1,466	612	2,819
	12,812	11,981	37	403	20	91	96	814	29	2,125
	3,080	977	157	80	99	11	170	310	177	307
	5,429	313	0	0	125	16	214	125	252	200
	1,154	14	0	1	0	*	0	5	0	2
	1,708	922	11	605	5	10	157	212	154	185
	7,715	23,211	3,410	5,584	1,077	368	2,727	5,746	2,851	3,241
	297	7,224	0	2,493	0	93	0	700	0	925
	4,687	4,902	2,950	923	375	76	1,735	700	1,785	1,000
	1,625	10,366	0	1,382	0	77	0	4,213	0	1,200
	1,106	719	460	786	702	122	992	133	1,066	116
	1,527	249	1	62	*	35	1	203	1	99
	144	71	*	3	*	*	*	3	*	3
	1,334	178	*	59	*	35	*	200	1	96
	49	0	*	0	*	0	*	0	1	0
	46,071	1,777	419	985	220	169	381	897	469	929
	22,508	1	0	0	0	0	0	0	0	0
	4,894	9	0	0	0	0	0	0	0	0
	1,834	77	65	90	38	3	57	65	41	35
	5,142	702	81	193	13	108	36	235	26	225
	8,911	348	187	622	136	36	158	305	280	350
	1,240	455	0	36	0	6	0	47	0	209
	1,059	46	23	30	22	3	47	91	41	50
	483	139	63	14	11	13	83	154	81	60
	2,663	1,043	139	78	37	21	184	107	160	127
	680	252	45	11	*	2	60	20	50	20
	1,443	733	82	58	35	18	104	75	84	96
	540	58	12	9	2	1	20	12	26	11
	1,070	457	104	274	36	71	150	216	169	122
	282	36	7	135	1	4	18	30	12	30
	217	343	31	125	*	*	31	30	46	32
	313	22	31	10	10	*	50	26	43	23
	258	56	35	4	25	67	51	130	68	37
	141	2,641	0	593	0	16	0	136	0	345
	123	1,267	0	534	0	9	0	62	0	178
	5	124	0	6	0	1	0	4	0	4
	13	1,250	0	53	0	6	0	70	0	163
	83,370	43,586	4,278	8,665	1,619	808	4,080	8,771	4,262	7,682

Notes for table 1-5.

Sources: AID, *U.S. Loans and Grants, July 1, 1945–June 30, 1975,* and *July 1, 1945–September 30, 1976;* and DSAA, *Foreign Military Sales and Military Assistance Facts, November, 1975,* and *December 1976.* Figures are rounded.

° Less than $0.5 million.

a. Includes security supporting assistance, military assistance program, foreign military sales credits, military assistance service funded grants, transfers of excess defense articles, and other grants, including ship loans.

b. Data available from 1950 onward; figures do not include foreign military sales credits.

c. Transitional budget, July 1–Sept. 30, 1976.

d. Belgium, Denmark, France, West Germany, Iceland, Italy, Luxembourg, Netherlands, Norway, Portugal, and the United Kingdom. Greece and Turkey, also NATO members, are shown separately.

e. Austria, Finland, Ireland, Malta, Spain, Sweden, and Switzerland; also includes security assistance to Berlin, 1946–65.

f. Includes $1.5 billion in arms sales for which payment was waived under the Emergency Security Assistance Act of 1973.

g. Bahrain, Egypt, Iraq, Jordan, Kuwait, Lebanon, Oman, Syria, and Yemen. Jordan is the major recipient in this group.

h. Nepal, Sri Lanka, and Afghanistan.

i. Includes general aid to Indochina, 1946–65.

j. Burma, Indonesia, Malaysia, and Singapore.

k. Only Nigeria and Tunisia received a total of more than $50 million in security assistance, 1946–75; Ghana, Liberia, Libya, Nigeria, South Africa, Tunisia, and Zaire were the only countries that purchased over $1 million in arms, 1946–75.

l. Figures exclude general costs and authorizations for international organizations (other than NATO) and for regional purposes.

CHAPTER TWO

Security Assistance

The shape of future U.S. security assistance programs began to emerge in the budget request for fiscal 1976. Two-thirds of the 1976 aid was programmed for Israel, Egypt, Jordan, and Syria; a similar preponderance was apparent in the 1977 and 1978 programs. Multiyear agreements to give aid in exchange for bases had been concluded with Spain, Turkey, and Greece and an agreement with the Philippines was being negotiated in 1978. These eight countries and South Korea accounted for more than four-fifths of the proposed 1978 program.

Half of the proposed 1978 funds were allocated as credits for government sales and more than two-fifths for economic aid in support of security budgets. The grant program providing military equipment, the traditional core of U.S. security assistance, had plummeted to less than 7 percent of the funds sought for fiscal 1978.[1] Though a number of countries are continuing to receive grants, the character and worldwide impact of equipment grants are changing fundamentally. The emphasis in grants for training is also changing; the military assistance advisory groups that had served around the world as advisers and as signs and channels of U.S. military interest were to be terminated by fiscal 1978 except where authorized for specific countries.

One early impact of the phasing out of the grant program has been on expectations abroad. It has at the very least put recipient countries on notice that assistance will not continue indefinitely. The case for continuance in many instances is marginal at best; the congressional direc-

---

1. U.S. Department of Defense, Defense Security Assistance Agency, "Security Assistance Program, Volume 1, FY 1978," Congressional Presentation (DSAA, 1977; processed), pp. 4–5.

tive in the International Security Assistance and Arms Export Control Act of 1976 serves as a means for officials at home and abroad to prepare clients for an early ending of grants. These countries, as a consequence, must begin to base their defense and budgetary planning on realistic estimates of what they can afford.

Origin and Evolution

The security assistance machinery that Congress began to dismantle in the 1970s is a complex series of programs that the secretaries of the Departments of State and Defense and the chairman of the Joint Chiefs of Staff consolidate and present annually, in the name of the President, as a comprehensive program important to the U.S. world role. It is a far more sophisticated vehicle of military aid than the first "foreign military assistance program" that was assembled by President Harry S. Truman.

Shortly before the ratification of the North Atlantic Treaty by the United States, on July 29, 1949, President Truman transmitted to Congress a special foreign aid bill that consolidated and expanded programs of military aid begun in the Philippines in 1946, in Greece and Turkey in 1947, and in China in 1948. A substantial consensus existed as to the objectives of the proposed program. The Senate Foreign Relations Committee saw it as "an essential step to carry forward the positive and vigorous action which the United States is taking in cooperation with other free nations to assure peace and security in the world."[2] The committee was aware that it would be very difficult to estimate military needs and costs, as well as to anticipate rates of economic recovery and the imminence and extent of military threats. Nevertheless, it declared that the United States should not commit itself to a program of "increasing dimensions" and that Congress should not feel bound to "future programs of similar character." In testimony before the committee, Secretary of Defense Louis Johnson hazarded the guess that military assistance would be needed for only four or five years and that the appropriations required to bring the program to an early conclusion would diminish each year.[3]

2. *Military Assistance Program*, S. Rept. 1068, 81:1 (GPO, 1949), pp. 3–5.
3. Ibid., p. 24. In section 405 of the draft legislation the committee stipulated that all or part of a program be terminated if a recipient requested that aid to it cease; if the aid were no longer consistent with the national interests

The new program was directed primarily toward Western Europe— tangible evidence of the importance assigned to the North Atlantic Treaty Organization (NATO). In the 1950s, as the military and foreign policy doctrine of containment was expanded to counter a worldwide Soviet threat, the assistance program was broadened. With the outbreak of hostilities on the Korean peninsula in 1950, the decision by President Gamal Abdel Nasser of Egypt in 1955 to turn to Czechoslovakia and the Soviet Union for arms, and the increasing U.S. role in Indochina, the geographic scope, the nature, and the immediate purposes of military assistance underwent changes. Defense of Northeast and Southeast Asia took on prominence; the criterion of "arms to allies" was enlarged to include "friends"; to the concepts of containment and forward defense were added new precepts of internal security, counterinsurgency, civic action, and nation building. The concept of containment, over a period of two decades, was expanded politically to apply to the protection not only of nations on the periphery of the Soviet Union, but of the world at large, including many nations regarded by their leaders as nonaligned.

The United States in 1978 was a participating member of four regional alliances[4] and was providing security assistance to fifty-seven countries. The original military aid legislation of 1949, the Mutual Defense Assistance Act, had been superseded by the Mutual Security Act of 1951, the Foreign Assistance Act of 1961, the Foreign Military Sales Act of 1968, and the International Security Assistance and Arms Export Control Act of 1976. In the process, military assistance had expanded into an elaborate security assistance program designed for transferring arms, providing security-related economic aid, and offering military technology and professional training.

The dollar level of U.S. contributions in goods and services to the defense capabilities of other nations has remained substantial—appropriations of $4.4 billion were requested for fiscal 1978. Between fiscal 1946 and 1976 these contributions totaled $97 billion (see table 1-4) and touched almost a hundred countries, the amounts ranging cumulatively from less than $100,000 (for Mauritius and Syria) to over $20 billion (for

---

of the United States or with the purpose and policies of the act; if such aid contravened a decision of the United Nations Security Council; if it violated the UN Charter obligations of the United States; or if there were a concurrent resolution by the two houses of Congress requiring termination (ibid., p. 34).

4. NATO, the Rio Treaty, Southeast Asia Treaty Organization (SEATO), and Australia–New Zealand–U.S. alliance (ANZUS).

South Vietnam). Over half the funds went to East Asia (including Southeast Asia). Europe, the major recipient in the 1950s, sank to second place in the early 1960s and now receives only minor amounts of aid. The only remaining major claimants after the end of the war in Indochina were Israel, Jordan, South Korea, Greece, Turkey, and Spain. Egypt and Syria fill out the list of current main claimants.

Military assistance through the years was complemented by economic assistance. During fiscal 1946–76, economic aid (apart from the supporting aid included in security assistance) totaled $95 billion, compared to the $97 billion in security aid. The annual obligations for each, in billions of dollars, in 1971–76 were:[5]

	1971	1972	1973	1974	1975	1976
Economic aid	2.9	3.3	3.5	3.3	3.7	2.8
Security aid	5.2	5.9	6.3	5.7	3.7	4.4

A succession of blue-ribbon commissions advising the President on foreign economic policy has considered the two programs in tandem.[6] In 1970 the Task Force on International Development headed by Rudolph Peterson suggested that the United States should reduce its role in determining the force structure and equipping of other countries' forces and encourage them "to estimate their own requirements, to relate them

5. U.S. Agency for International Development, *U.S. Overseas Loans and Grants and Assistance from International Organizations: Obligations and Loan Authorizations, July 1, 1945–June 30, 1976* (AID, 1977), p. 6.

6. The commission reports, and the designated chairman or principal adviser, are Gordon Gray, Special Assistant to the President, *Report to the President on Foreign Economic Policies* (GPO, 1950); *Partners in Progress, A Report to the President by the International Development Advisory Board* (GPO, 1951), Nelson Rockefeller, chairman; Commission on Foreign Economic Policy, *Report to the President and the Congress* (GPO, 1954), Clarence B. Randall, chairman; *Report to the President by the President's Citizen Advisors on the Mutual Security Program* (GPO, 1957), Benjamin Fairless, coordinator; *A New Emphasis on Economic Development Abroad,* A Report to the President of the United States (Washington: International Development Advisory Board, 1957), Eric Johnson; "Composite Report of the President's Committee to Study the United States Military Assistance Program" (Washington: The Committee; August 1959; processed), William Draper, chairman; "Report to the President of the United States from the Committee to Strengthen the Security of the Free World: The Scope and Distribution of United States Military and Economic Assistance Programs" (Department of State, March 1963; processed), Lucius Clay, chairman; and *U.S. Foreign Assistance in the 1970s: A New Approach,* Report to the President from the Task Force on International Development (GPO, 1970), Rudolph Peterson, chairman.

to their budgetary priorities, and to make their military decisions in the light of available resources." To further these aims it recommended that military assistance be shifted from a grant to a credit sales basis and the military assistance advisory missions in recipient countries be reduced.[7]

The Peterson Report reflected the increasing questioning of the security assistance program in the late 1960s. Congress in 1968, 1969, and 1970 made sharp cuts in the proposed budgets. In 1971 the Senate Foreign Relations Committee and the Joint Economic Committee conducted skeptical and probing hearings on military assistance.[8] In 1972 no authorizing legislation could be passed, and the program had to be funded by continuing resolution.

The Senate increasingly came to question the rationale and effectiveness of the military assistance program and voted in 1973 and 1974 to terminate the grant program for military equipment and the military assistance advisory groups by 1977. The Senate Foreign Relations Committee repeatedly urged that the United States provide grant military aid only in specific instances where assistance was clearly warranted, and not as a habit. The House International Relations Committee, generally more supportive of military assistance, was slow to join this effort. The House, though, was active in framing and imposing its position on particular issues on which it was at variance with the executive (for example, on the question of human rights and on Turkey's actions in Cyprus).

At the end of the Ninety-third Congress, in December 1974, funds had not been appropriated for security assistance (funds for South Vietnam were included in the U.S. defense budget) or for economic aid generally. Authorizing legislation had been passed that contained many restrictions related to general aspects of the program (such as draw-down authority and interest rates for credit sales) and particular recipients (for example, constraints on assistance for South Vietnam and Cambodia, suspension of aid and sales to Turkey, restrictions on aid to Chile and South

7. *U.S. Foreign Assistance in the 1970s*, Peterson Report, pp. 16–17. The only recommendation in the security assistance area that was adopted was the establishment by Congress of the position of under secretary of state for security assistance. The Commission on the Organization of the Government for the Conduct of Foreign Policy in its report by this same title (GPO, 1975), p. 80, recommended abolition of the position.

8. See *Economic Issues in Military Assistance*, Hearings before the Joint Economic Committee, 92:1 (GPO, 1971).

Korea). When funds were finally appropriated in March 1975, the security aid and aid to South Vietnam included in the defense program were cut from just under $4 billion proposed to a ceiling just over $3 billion.[9]

In early 1975, military assistance and sales to Turkey were suspended by congressional action following intervention of Turkish forces in Cyprus,[10] notwithstanding administration charges that the action injured NATO and Middle East security and prospects for a Cyprus settlement, and represented an unsound congressional intrusion into the conduct of foreign relations. Supplemental appropriations of $300 million for South Vietnam and $222 million for Cambodia were urgently (but fruitlessly) sought, with warnings to Congress that failure to provide the funds would be a default on U.S. moral obligations, lead to loss of South Vietnam to the Communists, and diminish U.S. credibility and effectiveness with allies and opponents alike. With the end of the conflict in Southeast Asia, the administration was faced with revamping its security assistance request for fiscal 1976, which in the budget submitted in February 1975 earmarked for Southeast Asia over $2 billion out of an overall program of $4 billion.[11] The Turkish aid dilemma, combined with a Middle East reappraisal and a new Southeast Asia position, delayed submission of the security assistance request until October 30, 1975. In the meantime a separate economic assistance bill was for the first time passed by the House Committee on International Relations, and subsequently by the full House and Senate.

In the spring of 1976, Congress passed the International Security Assistance and Arms Export Control Act of 1976. Despite close collaboration between the responsible committees and the staffs of the State and Defense departments during drafting of the legislation, it was vetoed by President Ford, primarily on grounds that the several provisions for congressional "reverse veto" on particular arms sales and country aid programs, by concurrent resolution, infringed on the President's constitutional prerogatives. The bill in somewhat modified form was reenacted and signed in June 1976. In this confrontation between Congress and the executive, the differences were related as much to prerogative as to substance.

9. 88 Stat. 1798–1812.
10. Ibid.
11. U.S. Office of Management and Budget, *Budget of the United States Government, Fiscal Year 1976* (GPO, 1975), pp. 83, 208–09, and 232.

The security assistance section of the 1976 act did two principal things: it decreed the termination, after fiscal 1977, of grant military assistance except for specific amounts authorized for specific countries and of military missions or advisory groups unless specifically authorized by Congress,[12] and it laid down procedures for terminating aid to countries that engage in practices that discriminate against U.S. citizens or that constitute a consistent pattern of gross violation of human rights.[13]

On both points, congressional sentiment had been hardening for years. Section 17 of the Foreign Assistance Act of 1974 had already stated the sense of Congress that the program of grants "should be reexamined in light of changes in world conditions and the economic position of the United States . . . and that the program, except for military education and training activities, should be reduced and terminated as rapidly as feasible consistent with the security and foreign policy requirements of the United States."[14] Congress had also been moving to achieve control and accountability over each element of the program. It asserted in successive authorizing and appropriation bills in the early 1970s its wish to be informed of all forms of security assistance, to authorize each and set fiscal and other limits, and to be informed and at times consulted on program execution; and it counterbalanced general authorizations with specific exceptions, restrictions, and conditions. In late 1975 the issue of congressional authority erupted dramatically with the discovery that military aid to factions in Angola was being drawn from Defense Department appropriations as a clandestine activity of the Central Intelligence Agency. Congressional determination to assert authority on such U.S. activities abroad was felt to be challenged. The 1976 act thus specified both the recipient countries and the share for each of grant military aid, with only narrow leeway for shifts by the executive.

The legislation also denied aid to governments that intern or imprison their citizens for political purposes. A coordinator of human rights and humanitarian affairs, in the Department of State, was made responsible for providing relevant information to assure that the U.S. policy of promotion and encouragement of respect for human rights and freedoms is not being disregarded and that security assistance is not given to countries engaged in a consistent pattern of gross violations; the coordinator was also required to explain extraordinary circumstances that

12. 90 Stat. 732.
13. 90 Stat. 748–53.
14. 88 Stat. 1800.

necessitate continuation of assistance in the face of human rights violations.

The Components of Security Assistance

Security assistance is the official term used by the executive to distinguish security-oriented components of the foreign aid program submitted annually to Congress for authorization and appropriation. The term has been in use since the President's Task Force on International Development in its 1970 report attempted to cluster all U.S. security-related assistance in one clearly designated category. In budget documents it includes grants for military materiel under the traditional military assistance program, grants for military training, funds for credits and guarantees for foreign military sales, and grants to foreign governments for support of their security programs. Data on these programs are presented in the foreign assistance budgets administered by the Department of Defense, the Agency for International Development (AID), and the Department of Agriculture. From 1966 until the end of hostilities in Southeast Asia, major additional funds for "military assistance service funded" grants were included in the Department of Defense budget for U.S. military forces.

The security assistance program is more than the sum of these parts, however. The picture of U.S. transfers of resources must be filled out with other categories, such as excess defense articles, ship loans, and emergency arms transfers under section 506 of the Foreign Assistance Act, as amended by the 1976 act.[15]

Military Assistance Program

The military assistance program was the centerpiece of the security-related foreign aid effort for a quarter of a century. The program has covered grants of military equipment, training, and other services. The purpose of such assistance has varied, depending on the particular situation in each recipient country, but, on the whole, each successive administration has justified the program in terms of defense and deterrence, internal stability and instability, and instruments to "strengthen the peace."

One of the original purposes of military assistance was to bolster the

15. 75 Stat. 436, and 90 Stat. 730.

Table 2-1. *Allocation of Proposed Budget for Military Assistance Program, by Purpose, Fiscal 1978*
Millions of dollars

Purpose	Amount	Percentage
Forward defense[a]	85.0	37.9
Base rights[b]	59.6	26.6
Other (political)[c]	79.5	35.5
Total	224.1[d]	100.0

Source: Calculated from U.S. Department of Defense, Defense Security Assistance Agency, "Security Assistance Program, Volume 1, FY 1978," Congressional Presentation (DSAA, 1977; processed), pp. 4–5.
a. Includes Greece, Turkey, and South Korea.
b. Includes Spain, Portugal, and the Philippines.
c. Includes Jordan, Indonesia, Thailand, Ethiopia, and six Latin American countries.
d. Excludes $60.6 million programmed for general costs.

combat capabilities of "forward-defense" countries on the periphery of the Communist world. Greece, Turkey, Iran, Pakistan, South Korea, and Taiwan received large amounts of forward-defense aid during the "containment" period. This means of lessening the likelihood of U.S. military involvement remains a vigorous part of the program, as table 2-1 shows.

Later, aid began to be offered in exchange for base rights. To maintain access to bases, and to gain overflight and other rights in support of U.S. defense requirements, large amounts of aid have been given to Portugal, Ethiopia, Libya, Spain, and the Philippines, as well as to Greece and Turkey. More recently, assistance has been given for political purposes to support the orderly political, economic, and social evolution of developing countries, to stabilize relationships among them, and to dispose them to support the objectives of U.S. foreign policy. In particular, military assistance has been used as a political instrument to gain and to maintain influence within the military establishments of selected countries, to help provide a military and paramilitary capability for internal security, and to maintain a balance of military forces in areas such as the Middle East. It has also been seen as a means of keeping other countries from replacing the United States as the major source of influence and support for military establishments (as in Latin America), of securing diplomatic or political leverage, and of funding UN peacekeeping forces.

The importance of U.S. military assistance to individual countries varies greatly. It was of great importance along with Marshall Plan economic aid to Western European countries at the time of the establishment and strengthening of NATO in the 1950s; it is now of only minor significance for NATO except for Greece and Turkey on the southern flank. In Latin America it is, with a few exceptions, small in proportion to total local military expenditures. In the period 1971–75, for example, Latin American military expenditures (omitting Cuba) totaled $20.8 billion; U.S. military assistance, including excess defense articles, totaled $564 million or about 2.7 percent of Latin American military budgets. Similarly, in Africa for the same period total military expenditures (omitting Egypt and South Africa) were $5.5 billion; U.S. military assistance and excess defense articles totaled $225 million or only 4.1 percent. At the other extreme, in East Asia (omitting Communist states) military expenditures for the period 1971–75 totaled $23.6 billion while U.S. security assistance totaled $17.2 billion or three-quarters of the total.[16] The budget request for fiscal 1978 showed a drastic decline in the amount of aid requested for East Asia as compared with authorizations in fiscal 1975 (see table 2-2). There was a large increase in the request for Europe, however, with $48 million proposed for Turkey, $33 million for Greece, $25 million for Portugal, and $15 million for Spain.[17]

While dollar values give some sense of the relative size of assistance programs, they do not describe the hardware that is involved. Under the military assistance program the United States had by the end of 1976 delivered to other governments approximately twenty-five thousand tanks, ten thousand combat aircraft, and over one hundred cruisers, destroyers, and submarines.[18] Between 1950 and 1976, more than half of the military assistance expenditures were on equipment, but over two-fifths went to such consumables and intangibles as ammunition, repair and rehabilitation, supply operations, training, and other services.[19] And in some years an even higher percentage of expenditures went into non-hardware aid—47.6 percent in fiscal 1971, for example.[20] Perhaps this was related to the use of sales and gifts of excess defense articles as the principal method for transferring major equipment and to emphasis in

16. Calculated from U.S. Arms Control and Disarmament Agency (ACDA), *World Military Expenditures and Arms Transfers, 1966–1975* (GPO, 1976); and AID, *U.S. Loans and Grants, July 1, 1945–June 30, 1975* (1976).

17. DSAA, "Security Assistance Program, Volume 1, FY 1978," p. 4.

18. DSAA, *Foreign Military Sales and Military Assistance Facts, December 1976* (DSAA, 1977), pp. 4–5.

19. Ibid., p. 3.

20. DSAA, "Military Assistance and Foreign Military Sales Facts, May 1973" (DSAA, 1973; processed), p. 7.

Table 2-2. *Allocation of Military Assistance Program, by Region,*
Fiscal 1970, 1975, and Proposed 1978
Millions of current dollars

	1970		1975		1978, proposed	
Region	Amount	Percentage	Amount	Percentage	Amount	Percentage
Near East and South Asia	112	31.0	74	13.4	55	24.5
East Asia[a]	185	51.3	428	78.0	47	20.9
Latin America	18	5.0	16	2.9	*	0.2
Africa	20	5.5	13	2.3	1	0.4
Europe	26	7.2	19	3.4	121	54.0
Total[b]	361	100.0	550	100.0	224	100.0

Source: U.S. Agency for International Development, *U.S. Overseas Loans and Grants and Assistance from International Organizations: Obligations and Loan Authorizations, July 1, 1945–June 30, 1975* (AID, 1976); and DSAA, "Security Assistance Program, Volume 1, FY 1978," pp. 4–5.
* Less than $500,000.
a. South Vietnam is not included in any of these allocations.
b. Excludes general costs.

budgeting on operations and maintenance because military assistance funds had declined. These percentages do not of course measure the investment in the reequipping and modernizing of forces or the cost of operations and maintenance, much of which is included under categories such as aircraft, vehicles, and weapons. The fiscal 1978 program envisaged an allocation of 69 percent to investment and 31 percent to operating costs and supply operations.[21]

Military Education and Training

Military education, training, and orientation were provided as part of military assistance until the passage of the International Security Assistance and Arms Export Control Act of 1976. The new international military education and training program grew out of an administration proposal in 1974 to separate training grants from assistance grants and provide a permanent program comparable to that provided under the Mutual Educational and Cultural Exchange Act of 1961 (the Fulbright-Hays act). Criticism had arisen in Congress over the burden of financing basic weapons and maintenance courses after twenty years of such instruction rather than shifting it to foreign military schools. And the long-term advantages of orientation visits and the like to the United States had come into question.

21. DSAA, "Security Assistance Program, Volume 1, FY 1978," p. 11.

Much of the program in the past was conducted by the Department of Defense at U.S. military installations, and training was provided by instructors stationed with U.S. military assistance advisory groups. In recent years, technical assistance field training teams have been sent to various countries for periods up to one year, and in some instances commercial firms have been hired to provide the training. In 1975, for instance, 9,535 people in one hundred and thirty-two technical assistance and training teams were serving in thirty-four countries under government contracts valued at $727 million. They ranged in size from one technician to several hundred people. Sixty teams (comprising the bulk of the personnel) were composed entirely of Defense personnel and sixty-seven of contractor personnel; five were mixed. The principal parties to these arrangements were South Vietnam, Saudi Arabia, and Iran.[22]

Training programs continue to be a strong part of security assistance under the 1976 act. A proposed budget of $35.7 million for such purposes in fiscal 1978 called for instruction for 5,267 foreign military and military-related personnel, representing forty-six countries.[23] The new act permits wide latitude in the planning and provision of training courses.

Security Supporting Assistance

Security supporting assistance is a supplement to military assistance, originally designed to maintain the economic and political stability of countries under stress or threat of conflict. Like military aid, it now serves a multiplicity of purposes. For several years the program has focused on the Middle East, a significant change from the years when Southeast Asia was the principal beneficiary (see table 2-3). By 1975 Secretary of State Kissinger, in his efforts to end hostilities in the Middle East, concluded that substantial economic aid should be available to parties to the negotiating process. Supporting assistance for Egypt and Syria as well as Israel and Jordan became an important vehicle for this purpose, as reflected in the fiscal 1976, 1977, and 1978 budget requests. Aid for other countries was made more specific: the Malta program represented the U.S. contribution to a NATO effort to insure a continued British military presence on the island and to preclude a comparable Soviet lodgment; aid for Portugal was to be used to retain U.S. access to Lajes airfield in the Azores and to encourage a moderate government in Lisbon.

22. *New York Times*, Feb. 20, 1975.
23. DSAA, "Security Assistance Program, Volume 1, FY 1978," pp. 12–15.

Table 2-3. *Distribution of Security Supporting Assistance,*
Fiscal 1970, 1975, and Proposed 1978
Millions of current dollars

Country	1970 Amount	1970 Per-centage	1975 Amount	1975 Per-centage	1978, proposed Amount	1978, proposed Per-centage
Cambodia	0	0	55	5.3	0	0
Egypt	0	0	253	24.2	750	42.3
Israel	0	0	325	31.1	785	44.3
Jamaica	0	0	0	0	10	0.6
Jordan	0	0	88	8.4	93	5.1
Laos	44	9.5	24	2.3	0	0
Malta	0	0	10	1.0	10	0.6
Nigeria	27	5.8	0	0	0	0
Portugal	0	0	15	1.4	0	0
South Korea	10	2.2	0	0	0	0
South Vietnam	361	77.6	188	18.0	0	0
Spain	0	0	3	0.3	7	0.4
Swaziland	0	0	0	0	11	0.6
Syria	0	0	83	8.0	90	5.1
Thailand	19	4.1	0	0	0	0
Zaire	0	0	0	0	10	0.6
Other	4[a]	0.8	0	0	8[b]	0.4
Total	465	100	1,044	100	1,774	100

Sources: AID, *U.S. Overseas Loans and Grants July 1, 1945–June 30, 1975;* and DSAA, "Security Assistance Program, Volume 1, FY 1978." Figures are rounded.
    a. Includes Guatemala, Haiti, and Mexico.
    b. Includes Botswana and Lesotho.

Sales Credits and Guarantees

Section 505c of the Foreign Assistance Act directs the President to shift progressively to developing countries more of the burden of their total defense costs as their economies grow. This has in fact been the trend for more than a decade. Iran, Taiwan, and other major recipients of military assistance in earlier years now rely on government-to-government and commercial sales to meet their equipment needs; military assistance was terminated for most of Western Europe in the 1960s. Moreover, today's recipients of grant aid are being slowly shifted to reliance on sales supported by government credit arrangements.

The transition from grants to credit sales does not shift a client state out of the aid category. Budgetary funds are required both to finance credits extended directly by the U.S. government and to underwrite commercial credit sales by guarantee; at least an opportunity cost to the American economy is involved, and an additional cost accrues to the

United States if the sales agreement provides for interest payments at less than the government would normally borrow money in the commercial marketplace. The shift to government-financed credit sales does, however, represent a substantial reduction in the U.S. contribution to the local defense costs of recipient countries, as well as a reduced budgetary burden to the United States as loans are repaid.

Excess Defense Articles

The secretary of defense has broad discretionary authority to reduce the Department of Defense's mobilization reserve requirements and declare portions of the equipment in its inventory to be excess.[24] Such articles located in the continental United States can be given to foreign governments and charged to the military assistance program at fair value (but not less than one-third their acquisition cost), and overseas stocks at varying values established by Congress. Between fiscal 1950 and 1976, transfers of $6.6 billion in excess stocks (at acquisition cost) were programmed;[25] the fiscal 1976 cost was $63 million.[26] For fiscal 1978 a proposed $10.0 million in excess equipment was to be used for security assistance.[27]

Ship Loans

The transfer to another country of any U.S. naval vessel in excess of two thousand tons or less than twenty years of age must be authorized by Congress; for other vessels, thirty days' notice of a proposed transfer must be given to the two armed services committees.[28] Before these restrictions were instituted in 1974, vessels stricken from the Naval Vessel Register and certified by the chief of naval operations as not essential to the defense of the United States could be transferred by the executive branch without congressional action or notification.

Some vessels are classified as excess defense articles, others as mobilization reserve. Those in the latter category are put on loan or lease to foreign countries, an arrangement the navy contends is less expensive than storage. Since these transfers are made on a long-term basis—only

24. 22 U.S. Code 2321b.
25. DSAA, *Foreign Military Sales and Military Assistance Facts, November 1975* (DSAA, 1976), p. 28.
26. DSAA, "Security Assistance Program, Volume 1, FY 1978," p. 17.
27. Ibid., p. 5.
28. 88 Stat. 406.

a handful of ships has actually been returned to U.S. control and of these only one or two in operable condition—they might properly be considered a form of nonreimbursable transfer comparable to transfers under the military assistance program.

Other Transfers

Section 506 of the Foreign Assistance Act permits the President to order defense articles from the stocks of the Department of Defense to be transferred for use under the grant military assistance program if he determines this to be in the security interest of the United States. Essentially, this is an emergency contingency fund, on which Congress has put a ceiling each fiscal year ($150 million for 1975; $67.5 million annually beginning in fiscal 1976).[29]

In unusual circumstances, Congress enacts special legislation for the transfer of American military equipment to other nations. For example, when the U.S. government informed the government of the Republic of Korea in July 1970 of its plans to reduce the number of American troops in South Korea substantially, it faced a choice of returning the equipment used by a deactivated division to the United States or transferring this materiel to the armed forces of South Korea. Congress, at the administration's request, enacted Public Law 91-652 in January 1971, authorizing the President to give to South Korea such U.S. military equipment located in that country "as he may determine."[30] The law neither imposed a limit on the amount or value of that equipment nor required that it be in excess of the requirements of U.S. forces in South Korea. In March 1971 $271 million in materiel (at acquisition cost) was turned over to South Korea in addition to the regular assistance for that fiscal year which was well over $100 million.[31]

Other specially legislated funds in the budget of the Department of Defense include major amounts appropriated to support the war efforts of countries in Southeast Asia and to pay the costs of U.S. military assistance missions and advisory groups. These military assistance special funds and security assistance supporting funds supplied budgetary, foreign-exchange, and other economic assistance to Southeast Asian

29. 87 Stat. 722; 88 Stat. 1798; 90 Stat. 730.
30. 84 Stat. 1942–43.
31. DSAA, *Foreign Military Sales and Military Assistance Facts, November 1975*, p. 29n.

countries that was continued as Indochina postwar reconstruction aid in the budgets for fiscal 1974 and 1975. Because of the intensity and costs of continued hostilities, the reconstruction funds were used to support the war effort and they can thus be regarded as security assistance.[32]

Shaping a Policy of Military Aid

The continuing debate over security assistance revolves around its use as an instrument of U.S. policy. During the years that Henry Kissinger served as secretary of state, it was the most prominent instrument of foreign policy. Military aid was considered vital to preserving ties with America's allies, forging more rational relationships with its adversaries, maintaining regional balances of power, and creating a new era of cooperativeness with all nations. Whatever the nature of the regimes it supported, security assistance was viewed as the first step toward a positive U.S. influence and as a hindrance to other, undesirable sources of supply.

But the Kissinger propositions offered little ground for discrimination, and critics of his policy suggested that security assistance ought to be one of the alternatives in an array of policy choices. It should be the policy followed only when it could be defended as wise for the United States, for the benefiting country, and for other countries affected by it. Assistance might buy only the illusion of influence. It could commit the United States to the further support, or even defense, of another country; certainly, if the United States views military help as a principal means of influencing countries, it opens itself to easy blackmail by them. It also could poison U.S. relations with neighbors or rivals of the recipient country.

At the least, it might be advantageous to the United States politically as well as fiscally to have other friendly countries share the burden of support. Security assistance may be justifiably given to help other states

32. The Food for Peace program under Public Law 480 has at times been used for security assistance purposes, particularly in Southeast Asia and the Middle East. In addition, until 1975, funds from local sales of Food for Peace could be used, with U.S. concurrence, for various local purposes including defense costs (68 Stat. 456); during the life of this stipulation, fiscal 1955–74, over $2 billion was used for local defense purposes in twelve countries. (DSAA, "Fiscal Year Series" [(1974); processed], p. 13.) These allocations are not included in security assistance totals in this study, though they do not differ in objective from security supporting assistance.

like Israel, South Vietnam, Cambodia, and South Korea maintain a capability to defend themselves; or make it possible for allies such as Greece and Turkey to contribute to a common defense effort with U.S. forces; or give confidence to nations such as South Korea, Israel, and Thailand in negotiations or other political adjustments. It may also be necessary in order to obtain leverage in pursuit of important U.S. diplomatic objectives, as in Middle East and Cyprus settlements; or to gain for the United States base and transit rights and access to local facilities, in normal times and emergencies, in Spain, Portugal, Turkey, or the Philippines; or to provide a symbol of U.S. commitment or concern for the security of recipient countries such as Israel and South Korea.

Further, it may be reasonably offered to politically or strategically important countries like Egypt and Indonesia as a means of limiting Soviet or other influence or dominance; sometimes, as in Turkey, South Korea, and Latin America, to influence the character, combat capabilities, and future roles of recipients' armed forces; or to maintain access and influence, as with military training grants, with key leaders and groups in recipient countries. It may be used to help defeat insurrection, insurgency, or guerrilla activity—as it has been in Jordan, Thailand, and Indonesia. Finally, security assistance might be used, as in South Korea, to give a would-be aggressor pause where the United States might otherwise have to use its own armed forces.

Deciding whether assistance should be continued, and how valuable past assistance has been,[33] is often complicated by a multiplicity of objectives. For example, Thailand still has not subdued its insurgency, but it provided bases and even active help to the United States during the Indochina hostilities, and it remains a factor in the regional political and power balance in Southeast Asia. Similarly, Turkey refused use of its facilities for resupplying Israel during the October 1973 war, and it used U.S. equipment in invading Cyprus in 1974, but for years it permitted the United States the use of intelligence facilities; moreover, it helps defend the southern flank of NATO. Indeed, though the ostensible purpose of aid may be the defeat of aggression or defense of a legitimate regime, the controlling factor may be a preference for conservative Arabs over

33. In 1971 the comptroller general of the United States, Elmer Staats, testified: "One of the most difficult problems we have in the GAO is to evaluate the effectiveness of our foreign assistance programs, both economic and military. My feeling is that about the only way that you can get at this is to have people who live very much with these programs. To some degree, it has to be subjective." *Economic Issues in Military Assistance*, Hearings, p. 75.

radical ones, a fear of "losing" the Dominican Republic, a distaste for Marxists and revolutionaries, or, most intangible of all, a determination to have our own way and not to be defeated once we have publicly taken sides, invested money, and spilt American blood.

But regardless of how attractive the reasons for providing security assistance may seem, certain practical tests should be met, and sound and desirable objectives identified. Will the assistance really achieve its purposes? For example, will training a few officers each year affect the political orientation of even a military regime? Will the supply of military equipment and money lead to self-reliance or to dependence on U.S. supplies? Also, are the likely results worth the costs? What effects of U.S. involvement ought to be anticipated? Will U.S. aid to a state improve its position or be followed by an offsetting strengthening of its internal or external opponents? Will U.S. involvement give greater and broader significance to a local conflict, and lead to counterbalancing involvement by other major powers? How will U.S. involvement affect the political situation and tone of the recipient regime? Will it enhance confidence, unity, and resolve, or tag the regime as foreign backed and lead to a feeling that responsibility is now in U.S. hands?

In evaluating the significance of security assistance, there is often a tendency to pass over other U.S. influences that also may be at play. It is plausible that U.S. aid has been indispensable to the survival of nations that are not formal allies of the United States, such as Israel and Jordan, and for several years South Vietnam. But given U.S. treaty commitments and the deployment of the Sixth and Seventh Fleets and other U.S. forces, was assistance critical to the survival of Turkey, Taiwan, and Thailand, or even important to "helping them defend themselves" against such presumed opponents as the Soviet Union and China? Did Indonesia turn to the United States for help and support because some officers of the new military regime remembered their U.S. training, or primarily because of all that the United States had to offer politically, economically, technically, and militarily and because of disillusion with the communist powers? Does U.S. influence in Latin America rest to a significant degree on ties of military aid? Military assistance is important, but it must be looked at in proportion, and as one of the many ways in which the United States interacts with other countries.

On occasion U.S. interest in security and stability is at odds, in relation to a particular country, with other U.S. goals. Aid for economic development may deserve priority in the allocation of U.S. resources. Food for

Peace may be needed in famine-stricken nations rather than one where the United States has an immediate security interest. In developing countries, U.S. arms aid and purchases could have harmful economic consequences. The U.S. objective of reordering the world economy and its trade and financial institutions is today second to none in importance. Similarly, U.S. interest in human rights and in working with democratic or nonrepressive regimes has also become stronger; these concerns may eventually displace security objectives as a controlling factor in dealing with countries such as the Philippines and even South Korea.

And the overriding objective of international peace and order, while a justification for aid to UN forces in Korea and Cyprus, and to both sides of the contest in the Middle East, may in some circumstances rule out security assistance. In local conflicts, U.S. aid can contribute to power-bloc politics, make the opponents of U.S.-backed states more dependent on communist backing (as North Vietnam relied on the USSR and China), make regional efforts to end a conflict more difficult, and even perpetuate the suspicion that the United States applies one law for the strong and another for the weak.

Security assistance contributes to the recipient nation's independent capability of action. Like the Soviet Union in Indonesia, Ghana, and Egypt, the United States has suffered resounding setbacks in areas where it has given aid—for example, in Libya, in Cuba, and in Ethiopia —and has been treated with disdain by France, Greece, and Turkey despite massive aid programs. U.S. arms were used by Turkey in invading Cyprus, by Pakistan and India in their clashes, and by military rebels in seizing power in Latin America. It is prudent to wonder whether successors to the regimes in Iran and a number of Arab states that have been given or sold arms—Jordan and Saudi Arabia, for example—will be hostile to the United States, and whether the ambitions of the shah of Iran are congruent with U.S. interests and objectives.

Defense and International Security

Whatever the general foreign policy rationale for security assistance, the basic defense purpose will be to help other countries to defend themselves. Few of the forward-defense countries that were once given military assistance because of their proximity to the Sino-Soviet bloc remain in the program. Greece (despite its inclusion in the fiscal 1978 proposal),

Iran, and Taiwan no longer meet the means test. Pakistan has received few U.S. arms since the 1967 war with India. The countries of Southeast Asia received massive aid well into 1975, but for reasons better described as self-determination than containment. Thailand still receives aid—no longer for its base facilities, but for its perceived key role in the region and to combat insurgency.

Only South Korea and Turkey continue in the aid program because of an adjacent Communist threat. In South Korea the issue is complicated by the presence of U.S. troops and their complex mission (both local and regional), the uncertain prospects for improved relations with North Korea, and the tense domestic political situation.

In Turkey, aid is justified as a NATO requirement. Yet the case for helping Turkey maintain a larger military establishment than it can afford needs to be reexamined. Whether Turkey can help deter a Soviet attack rests on its will to resist, and on the strength of U.S. NATO forces having bases in Turkey and with the Sixth Fleet in the Mediterranean. The current readiness of Turkish forces seems to be more pertinent to the protection of Turks in Cyprus against Greek forces than to the deterrence of the Soviet Union.

The security assistance programs for both South Korea and Turkey now concentrate on providing new equipment rather than on supporting operations and maintenance. This is not only good military policy, but sound budgetary policy. Making Turkey and South Korea pay the operating and maintenance costs of their armed forces puts on them the onus for deciding how large their forces should be. The United States can concentrate on modernization, and when it ends the assistance program the shock will not be severe.

South Korea is now the only country receiving security assistance to offset a reduction in U.S. troops stationed there to assure the nation's survival. In 1977 President Carter determined that the more than thirty thousand U.S. ground troops deployed in South Korea should be withdrawn by 1982. United States Air Force units are to remain in South Korea indefinitely, however. Security assistance for Turkey, where no major U.S. combat forces are stationed, has been keyed largely to the United States' NATO obligations and buys the right to use Turkish facilities for transit, intelligence, and so forth. The right to be present (for example, in Spain and the Philippines as well as in Greece, Turkey, and the Azores) is now the more common purpose of security assistance.

Though security assistance can buy bases and facilities, it cannot assure they will be available in a crisis, as the United States learned in Spain, Greece, and Turkey during the 1973 Middle East war. Before paying a high price—politically as much as financially—the United States should calculate when and under what circumstances the facilities would be crucial and whether they can realistically be expected to be available. Reassessment of the usefulness of a costly base may turn up other technical possibilities or other locations, including U.S.-based operations, thus sparing the United States the kind of consequences it faced in Ethiopia and Thailand.

An alternative to the barter arrangement is the straightforward payment of rental or use charges, funded through the Department of Defense budget. However, where the interest of the host country in striking the best possible bargain is likely to lead to its politicizing the transaction, the item should probably continue to be put up to Congress in the security assistance budget—as is the case for Spain, for example—rather than risk charges of being hidden in the Defense budget.

The United States has not only supplied military equipment to fight insurgency in Thailand, but also to help resolve internal problems in the Philippines, Indonesia, and Latin America. Yet, supporting a country facing insurrection—and where that insurrection may be aided from outside by a major adversary of the United States—raises sharp question. An outbreak of internal violence and dissent may in fact be a check against economic and social progress, but it may be simply a normal convulsion in the process of change. If an indigenous revolutionary movement has the vitality to sustain itself, U.S. involvement with a beleaguered regime could rebound and enhance the nationalist credentials of the rebels. The internal security problems of other nations can best be dealt with by the local authorities.

The United States has also used military assistance to shape the structure, equipment, and doctrine of the armed forces of nations that might engage in hostilities jointly with U.S. forces in order to assure compatibility among alliance forces. These are reasonable desiderata for grants; they are hardly independent justification for aid. Still another objective of assistance in the future might be "to permit the recipient country to participate in collective measures requested by the United Nations for the purpose of maintaining or restoring international peace and security."[34] Such stabilization in the past has been to the U.S. interest.

34. Section 502 of the Foreign Assistance Act, originally section 505 (75 Stat. 436).

Political Objectives

For as long as the security assistance program has been in existence, it has been used to obtain political ends. Congress, for example, has enacted penalties to discourage uncompensated nationalization of U.S. property (in the Hickenlooper amendment to the 1962 aid authorization act), excessive defense expenditures or purchases of sophisticated weapons (in the Symington and Conte-Long amendments to the 1967 aid authorization and appropriations bills, respectively), seizure of U.S. fishing boats (in the 1972 Pelly amendment to the Fishermen's Protective Act of 1967), violation of human rights (in the fiscal 1975 aid authorization bill), unauthorized use of aid materiel by Turkey (in the fiscal 1975 continuing appropriations and aid authorization acts).

Foreign military and economic aid is a tempting device for Congress as well as for the executive branch, as an instrument for showing favor or disfavor, or to provide incentive or penalty. Earlier executive aid requests for the military government in Chile, and the congressional rejection of most of them reflect sharply opposed judgments of that regime, but similar attitudes as to an appropriate way to use foreign aid. The inclusion of Portugal in the Foreign Assistance Act of 1975 as it began to give up its African colonies and appeared to be making a step toward democracy, and the conditional authorization of some funds for military assistance for South Korea related to easing of internal political repression[35] are other cases of the "reward and punishment" approach. There are cases when it is sound or unavoidable, but it is a shallow and vulnerable basis for any substantial or continuing program.

Judicious use of assistance for political purposes can be good diplomacy. It works when the aid helps the recipient do what he wants or finds to be in his own interest (for example, enabling a moderate Arab ruler, such as Hussein in Jordan, to survive) or when it is distributed among antagonists (to facilitate negotiations between Israel, Egypt, and Syria). The use of aid as pressure, blackmail, or penalty has had mixed success— the Hickenlooper, Pelly, and Conte-Long amendments had no measurable effect either as warnings or as sobering penalties, and efforts to use delays on security assistance to soften tough Israeli negotiating positions have either had limited success or have had to be coupled with massive aid commitments.

35. 88 Stat. 1816–17 and 1802.

Trying to buy anything that carries political costs also raises difficulties, for the value of security aid can be limited or illusory. When the United States seeks to have its clients (Greece and Turkey) stay in an alliance, or out of the Communist orbit, or reject leftist regimes that are opposed to U.S. economic interests (as in Chile, Bolivia, and Malta), or when it needs facilities or overflight rights (as in Spain, Portugal, Turkey, Greece, and Thailand) or attempts to gain influence, a respectful hearing, and good relations (as in Indonesia, Egypt, and Brazil), the other party rather quickly understands that it has the upper hand in the bargaining.

The United States is in a weak position to either reduce its aid or demand compliance with the stated purposes for which it is given as long as, for example, it is more important to the United States than to Greece and Turkey that they stay in NATO and it is obvious that they can demand a high price for bases, political orientation, or easy relations. It will not be unnoticed if the United States fails to use its leverage when a client overtly refuses to permit use of facilities in critical operations such as the resupply of Israel during the October 1973 war (when Turkey permitted Soviet overflight); or uses grant equipment contrary to contractual purposes (as Turkey did in Cyprus) or in activities the United States deplores (such as the 1967 military coup in Greece and the Greek junta's involvement in the 1974 coup against Archbishop Makarios).

The United States may have to use security assistance for political ends, particularly in negotiating for bases or other facilities or access rights that have to be bought from another member of an alliance. If payment is calculated on grounds that a U.S. presence carries domestic or foreign political costs and risks for the host country, that should be the warning signal for a tough reassessment of the U.S. need for the facility: first, to weigh its value against its cost, and second to judge the likelihood that it will be available in a crisis, if pressure should be put on the host to stay neutral. When alliance or other political commitments or influence and good relations are put on the auction block, the United States should remember that its support and goodwill are in themselves of great security and economic value and question whether paying for these commodities gains anything beyond the likelihood of having to continue to pay. The political value of security assistance should be regarded as neither even nor predictable.

At times the United States may wish to employ sanctions against a nation whose security it is interested in but whose actions conflict with the general U.S. interest in personal freedom and representative government and repugnance for persecution and violent repression. There may be cases in which the offending country has such special ties to the United States or is the victim of so flagrant an aggression that the character of the current regime has little weight. Sanctions, including use or threat of aid cutoffs or reduction, may be ineffective, and may well harm the people who are the victims of repression, rather than the regime they are aimed at, particularly where U.S. economic aid emphasizes development activities directed to the poorest strata of society. Since military assistance can actually strengthen, or appear to strengthen, the capacity of a regime that rules by force to retain its authority, cutting off this aid can serve to distance the United States from a repressive regime—as it has with Chile. If sanctions are judged in a particular case to be the right course for the United States, cutting off military aid does not hurt the people and it hits the instruments and status symbols of the regime itself.

The United States cannot dictate to other countries what kind of government or leaders they should have, and it should not try to do so, openly or covertly. Normal diplomatic and commercial relations are in order with any regime in the absence of active hostility or exceptional viciousness. Aid, however, represents substantial support, and is a symbol of some mutual interest. Unless it is very clear what that interest is, the United States should refrain from providing security assistance, particularly to a regime that is not merely authoritarian, but actively and cruelly repressive. Though determination of violations of human rights may be difficult to make, the United States must take the time to reach a judgment where rights are in dispute; otherwise, U.S. purposes in granting assistance will be subject to misrepresentation at home and abroad.

President Carter's concern to "promote and advance respect for human rights" through the security assistance program[36] was reflected in reductions of the funds designated in the fiscal 1978 budget proposal for Argentina, Uruguay, and Ethiopia. The decision not to lessen the amount designated for South Korea on this same ground as a result of security considerations caused consternation among many because of the inconsistency. This is bound to occur, though, when cases involving differing and, to varying degrees, conflicting interests present themselves. Examining and debating the wisdom of the individual judgments that are made will be more useful than searching for simple consistency.

36. "Conventional Arms Transfer Policy: Statement by the President, May 19, 1977," *Weekly Compilation of Presidential Documents*, vol. 13 (May 23, 1977), p. 757.

CHAPTER THREE

Arms Sales

Though the U.S. approach to arms transfers has been dominated by political and security considerations, it has also included an economic and commercial element. Defense production is a substantial sector of the economy, and arms exports are significant—foreign sales deliveries of defense articles and services, government and commercial, totaled over $4 billion in fiscal 1976.

Within the executive branch until 1977 there was a strong group of proponents of arms sales who favored a policy of open access on a commercial basis. Along with a number of members of Congress they welcomed sales as a shot in the arm to the economy, a help in maintaining a favorable balance of trade, a way of recovering dollars spent on oil imports, and a factor in holding down unit costs of weapons procured for U.S. forces.

Those on the opposite side in Congress, who have long viewed arms sales with alarm, now have allies in the executive; they see arms sales as dangerous for world and regional stability and peace, wasteful for the purchasing countries, and often risky for the United States. President Carter, in his May 1977 statement on arms transfers, spoke of the world arms traffic as endangering "stability in every region of the world" and as a "threat to world peace."[1] The Senate Appropriations Committee, among the most forceful advocates of restraint during the Nixon and Ford administrations, in its report on the foreign aid bill of 1974 urged that "the arms we transfer to other countries must clearly be needed to

1. "Conventional Arms Transfer Policy: Statement by the President, May 19, 1977," *Weekly Compilation of Presidential Documents*, vol. 13 (May 23, 1977), p. 756.

counter a realistic threat."[2] It went on to ask that the fiscal 1976 request for credit appropriations for foreign military sales include a detailed discussion of the problems and prospects for conventional arms control agreements; evaluation of the impact of U.S. credits on regional arms races; and summaries of discussions on arms control with proposed recipients of U.S. credit and with other arms suppliers.

Congress as a whole has taken a less extreme view of arms sales, as both the Foreign Military Sales Act of 1968 and the International Security Assistance and Arms Export Control Act of 1976 indicate. Arms sales are seen as primarily of political and military significance, rather than economic. They are seen as having possible benefits for the recipient, but also possible drawbacks and risks for the United States, which impose a need for careful and balanced administration of government sales and careful regulation of commercial sales. The provision of arms is considered to be desirable or mutually convenient in certain instances, but those instances are expected to be considered in terms of a range of specific criteria against which every proposed transfer is to be examined before approval.

Legislation Pertaining to Sales

The effort by Congress to intervene in arms sales provoked President Gerald Ford in May 1976 to veto a bill regulating both gifts and sales of arms to foreign governments. The veto was aimed at Congress's right to block certain transactions by concurrent resolution, a right that "would seriously obstruct the exercise of the President's constitutional responsibilities for the conduct of foreign affairs."[3] The President also attacked the "arbitrary" ceiling of $9 billion placed on arms sales on the grounds that it would prevent U.S. industry from competing fairly and limit the United States' ability to meet the legitimate defense needs of friends. A new version of the bill, without a ceiling on sales and with a softened provision on congressional oversight, was signed by President Ford in June 1976.

2. *Foreign Assistance and Related Programs Appropriations Bill,* S. Rept. 94-39, 94:1 (GPO, 1975), p. 126.
3. "Veto of Foreign Assistance Bill," *Weekly Compilation of Presidential Documents,* vol. 12 (1976), p. 830.

The International Security Assistance and Arms Export Control Act of 1976[4] brings together the regulations governing public and commercial sales of arms abroad. The provisions relating to government sales are essentially those contained in the Foreign Military Sales Act of 1968,[5] and those regulating commercial exports are a continuation of rules set out in the Mutual Security Act of 1954.[6] Even the controversial right of Congress to block sales is not new, having been established in 1974 by the Nelson amendment to the Foreign Military Sales Act.[7]

One important change in the governance of arms transactions lies in the thrust of the 1976 legislation. Clearly, Congress wishes to see more careful weighing of pros and cons in executive branch decisions, and it has not only assumed the authority to impose its judgments on the merits of major proposed sales but now requires a timely flow of information on arms sales from the executive.

Sales of arms by the government to "friendly countries" are, by law, to be made "solely" to meet their requirements for internal security, legitimate self-defense, participation in UN or other collective peacekeeping measures, and civic action. The President, furthermore, must find that the sale will strengthen U.S. security and promote world peace. Export licenses for commercial sales of major defense equipment may not exceed $25 million, except for equipment sold to NATO countries. Generally, large sales are to be handled on a government-to-government basis.

Before a sale is approved, consideration must be given to possibilities that the equipment might contribute to an arms race, increase the possibility of outbreak or escalation of conflict, or prejudice development of bilateral or multilateral arms arrangements. Sales are not to be approved, except on waiver by the President, to countries ruled by military dictators unresponsive to social needs.

Sales are prohibited to countries that discriminate against U.S. citizens, and U.S. agencies and contractors are barred from acceding to discrimination. Although the President may waive this requirement on the grounds of national interest, Congress may override the waiver by joint

4. 90 Stat. 729–69.
5. 82 Stat. 1320.
6. 68 Stat. 832.
7. 88 Stat. 1814.

resolution. Any sale that adversely affects U.S. combat readiness requires presidential justification and certification.

Over the years the basic purposes of arms sales and the criteria for judging them have changed little. The executive branch is responsible for management of sales, and most of the limitations may be set aside by presidential waiver on security grounds. Congress must take the initiative, and obtain a majority of both houses, to stop a sale. However, any proposed arms sale of $25 million or more, or of major defense equipment valued at $7 million or more, must be reported to Congress, which can act within thirty calendar days to block it by concurrent resolution.

Every sales contract, government or commercial, must include a provision reserving the U.S. government's right to cancel all or any part of an order prior to delivery of goods or services. Foreign countries are not allowed to purchase excessive or sophisticated military equipment that would compete for resources needed for economic development or occasion diversion of economic aid. Moreover, sales are not to be made to Communist countries or those under Soviet domination or to countries that have violated earlier contracts. Arms are not to be retransferred to a third country without U.S. consent and must be used for the purposes for which the United States furnished them. They must also be given security protection.

Information on arms sales or export licenses must be unclassified unless its disclosure would be "clearly detrimental" to U.S. security. The director of the Arms Control and Disarmament Agency must be consulted regarding export licenses, and the reports to Congress on prospective major sales are to include an analysis of their impact on arms control.

The executive branch routinely applies several other tests to arms sales. The Department of State, for example, attempts to insure that sales do not contravene international efforts the United States supports (for instance, the UN embargoes directed against South Africa and Rhodesia), or obligations under international agreements (such as the limited test ban and nonproliferation treaties), or U.S. policy restrictions (like the embargo on shipping lethal weapons to India and Pakistan). Sensitive weapons like hand-carried missile launchers, which would be especially dangerous if they fell into terrorist hands, or weapons primarily for use against crowds are presumed to be unsatisfactory for export. And in countries where there is a U.S. military advisory group, it must judge whether the purchaser will be able to handle and maintain the equipment it wishes to buy.

Applying Legislation on Arms Sales

The clear-cut statutory delineations of states eligible for sales, of restrictions on transfer and use of weapons, and of U.S. international obligations and policies that limit arms transfers are criteria that can be easily applied in judging the wisdom of proposed sales. Determining whether those sales are for valid defense requirements, likely to advance U.S. security and world peace, economically sound, conducive to arms control and regional stability, and not a buttress for repressive regimes is not simple.

What to some observers appears to be an intolerable degree of domestic repression by a military regime is to others regrettable but not so troublesome as to prevent arms sales that are expected to encourage politically desired alignments or maintain a regional power balance. Military expenditures or arms purchases that to some are inexcusably wasteful of resources of foreign exchange will be judged by others to be understandable decisions indicative of national priorities. Acquisitions of advanced equipment in the Persian Gulf or Latin America will be assessed by some not as justified by legitimate threats to national survival and security, but as motivated by rivalry or emulation or by a desire for prestige, in what amounts to an arms race, while others will see the military buildup as strengthening self-defense capabilities and supporting regional stability.

It was such differences in perspective that marked the controversy over the 1976 legislation governing arms transfers. There was an uneasy sense that too many arms were being sold by the United States and other countries. There was skepticism that arms sales could be counted on to advance international security or U.S. influence. There was doubt that proper weight was being given in arms sales decisions and activities to arms control possibilities, human rights violations, and discrimination and the dangers of international terrorism. There was also recognition that individual decisions are difficult and that policies and programs capable of effecting a transformation in the arms trade have still to be devised.

The arms transfer policy that Secretary of State Kissinger subscribed to was based on the belief that world order rests on a regional as well as a global balance of power and that military power if controlled by the United States is inherently stabilizing, internally as well as internationally. Supplying arms to other nations is thus presumptively constructive rather than of neutral or negative effect. Kissinger and Secretary of Defense Schlesinger believed that other suppliers would come forward if the United States refrained from selling arms. They advocated that the United States be the supplier because of the political influence and diplomatic and military access that sales would bring. Forgoing such influence and access would not only be a loss, but a loss compounded if a rival was thus enabled to invade a U.S. zone of influence.

The economic burden of arms or the risk attending arms buildups in the Third World were thus issues that did not preoccupy the Ford administration. Its route to stability and construction of an international system enabling a "generation of peace" was through settlement of conflicts and issues, political agreements and structures, rather than through arms limitations or lowered military expenditures. Arms controls or reductions were viewed as elements or consequences of political developments, and of changed power relationships, rather than as instruments for political change.

To the Senate Foreign Relations Committee, which expressed the view that "United States policies should be geared to restricting, not expanding, the world arms trade," the administration's actions appeared to be "a pitch to nations around the globe."[8] But the executive branch did not subordinate foreign policy considerations to the promotion of arms sales. It simply held a different view of the foreign policy weight of arms sales. The administration did not express concern about the world's arms burden, except with regard to the strategic arms race; nor did it promote arms sales except to advance foreign policy and international interests as it saw them.

The wisdom of using arms sales as a regular instrument of foreign policy came under direct attack early in the Carter administration. In May 1977 the President made a formal statement of his policy on arms transfers. He declared his intention of reducing immediately the dollar volume of new commitments for foreign military sales and assistance; programs for "weapons and weapons-related items in FY 1978 will be reduced from the FY 1977 total." He promised that the United States would not be "the first supplier to introduce into a region newly developed, advanced weapons systems which would create a new or significantly higher combat capability." Nor would it permit such systems

8. *Foreign Assistance Act of 1974: Report of the Committee on Foreign Relations*, S. Rept. 93-1299, 93:2 (GPO, 1974), pp. 62–64.

to be developed or significantly modified solely for export. For certain weapons, equipment, or major components, transfers to third parties might be forbidden. And activities to promote sales abroad would require "policy-level authorization by the Department of State."[9]

These stipulations were to apply to transactions with all nations except those with which the United States maintained "major defense treaties"—the NATO countries, Japan, Australia, and New Zealand. However, the United States would "remain faithful to our treaty obligations, and . . . assure the security of . . . Israel." In "extraordinary circumstances" a presidential exception might allow transfers of arms where "countries friendly to the United States must depend on advanced weaponry to offset quantitative and other disadvantages in order to maintain a regional balance."[10]

This announced change in policy brought the administration much closer to the legislative position than the executive had been in recent years. But the Carter administration in its first year had a questionable record of following its own strictures. Shortly after President Carter announced his policy, requests by Iran and Pakistan to buy combat aircraft valued at $4 billion and $0.5 billion, respectively, were turned down.[11] By the end of the summer, however, the administration had sent to Congress forty-five requests for arms sales totaling $4.1 billion. Less than one-tenth of this amount was for sales to NATO nations, Japan, Australia, and New Zealand.[12] Moreover, three-quarters of the total value of U.S. arms sales made in fiscal 1977—including roughly eight months while the Carter administration was in office—were estimated to have gone to Iran, Saudi Arabia, and Israel.[13]

There is no reason to doubt the administration's belief in the general value and utility of a restrictive arms sales policy. But the new administration's interpretation of U.S. interests is in many ways similar to that of its predecessor. It is unlikely that the performance of the Ford and Carter

9. "Conventional Arms Transfer Policy."

10. Ibid.

11. Bernard Weinraub, "U.S. Withholds Sale of Jets to Pakistan," *New York Times*, June 3, 1977, and "U.S. Said to Bar Sale of 250 Jets Ordered by Iran," *New York Times*, June 8, 1977.

12. Herbert Y. Schandler and others, "Implications of President Carter's Conventional Arms Transfer Policy" (Congressional Research Service, 1977; processed), pp. 26–29.

13. Harold J. Logan, "Bureaucracy Still Struggling to Restrain U.S. Arms Sales," *Washington Post*, Nov. 12, 1977.

administrations on the issue of arms sales will be dramatically different. Already the Carter administration has found itself supporting arms sales in furtherance of treaty commitments (to South Korea), to retain good relations with countries holding important assets (Iran), to fulfill commitments made in return for base rights (Spain), and to support Israel. As the producer of the largest array of advanced arms and military technology in the world, the United States will continue to be faced with requests from a large number of nations to purchase armaments on a regular basis.

Pressures toward a Liberal Sales Policy

Foreign arms sales continue to be valued by many Americans as a means of reducing the cost of arms to the U.S. defense budget: "An $8 billion sales program will, on the average, generate $560 million in cost savings annually"—an average of $7 million saved by the United States for every $100 million in foreign arms sales.[14] Foreign sales allow the Defense Department to defray a portion of its costs on research and development of weapons systems and other military equipment, since an R&D surcharge is a standard element of the purchase price of weapons systems sold to foreign nations, and receipts from it average 4 percent of sale prices.

Foreign orders also contribute to economies of scale in production whose benefits are passed on to all buyers, and they absorb part of the fixed overhead costs of production (for example, the costs of facilities and of design staffs). Moreover, arms sales to foreign nations decrease the likelihood of major gaps in production lines, which too may lower unit costs of weapons, and they may even keep open lines that the U.S. Department of Defense would pay dearly to reopen intermittently.

There is nothing to suggest that a policy of restraint on the part of the United States would be viewed by the Soviet Union and its arms-producing allies, or France, or other nations in the West as a model to be followed rather than as a unique opportunity to obtain new influence and customers. When Congress prevented major U.S. arms transfers to Latin

14. "Budgetary Cost Savings to the Department of Defense Resulting from Foreign Military Sales," staff working paper (Congressional Budget Office, May 24, 1976; processed), p. 1; also see David L. Morse, "Foreign Arms Sales: 2 Sides to the Coin," *Army*, vol. 26 (January 1976), pp. 14–21.

America in the late 1960s and early 1970s, Latin nations simply turned to European suppliers and the USSR. This experience could be repeated elsewhere, with U.S.-produced aircraft and missiles replaced by those of the United Kingdom, France, West Germany, and the USSR. France has indicated that it will not follow a U.S. lead in restricting arms sales; it is extremely questionable whether the USSR will do so either.[15]

"Actual reductions in the worldwide traffic in arms," as President Carter recognized, "will require multilateral cooperation." But if cooperation is not forthcoming, the turning away of sales—especially when the purchasers can turn to more willing suppliers—would certainly be interpreted by many Americans as a disregard for losses of jobs and corporate profits.[16] Moreover, certain corporations—especially those in the aerospace industry—might suffer significantly; they and their employees and affected communities would undoubtedly be strong lobbyists for larger foreign sales. Sober academic analysts may also seek an open sales policy as the means of forcing purchasing states to assume responsibility for their arms programs and of depoliticizing the U.S. interest in arms trade. On the other hand, U.S. restraint might spur the further development of arms industries in other countries.

It is noteworthy that economic objectives are absent from U.S. legislation governing arms sales abroad. However, the comprehensive study of sales policies and practices that the 1976 arms export control act called for was expected to consider the economic impact on foreign countries of U.S. arms sales policies and to determine "the benefits to the United States of such arms sales." Impacts on U.S. trade, the balance of payments, and employment in the United States were also to be examined.[17]

Of course, production and delivery of arms to foreign nations during the next several years would be only minimally affected by a more restrained executive policy now. The dollar value of U.S. government sales already in the production and delivery pipeline in 1977 was estimated at $32 billion, or equal to roughly three years worth of agreements.[18] If

15. New York Times, Nov. 23, 1977.

16. Foreign military sales were projected in 1977 to provide employment for approximately 350,000 U.S. workers during the next five years. International Security Assistance Act of 1977, H. Rept. 95-274, 95:1 (GPO, 1977), p. 29.

17. 90 Stat. 735 and 748.

18. Arms Transfer Policy, report to Congress for use of the Senate Foreign Relations Committee (GPO, 1977), p. 57.

delivery of these arms is not impeded, even firm application of a restrictive policy would not affect the quantity and quality of U.S.-made armaments transferred to foreign hands for years to come. Meanwhile, refusals to sell arms could have important ramifications for U.S. relationships with foreign nations. As the Carter administration deals with these dilemmas, its actions are likely to antagonize members of Congress who supported its restrictive policy as well as the opponents of arms transfer restrictions.

Regulating Commercial Sales

Little comprehensive information is available about commercial arms sales agreements with foreign nations—that is, sales made by U.S. corporations directly to other countries under license by the Department of State's Office of Munitions Control. A record of commercial military sales deliveries abroad is available, however. In fiscal 1971–75, deliveries totaled $2.3 billion or 22 percent of U.S. government sales deliveries. Commercial deliveries were 29 percent of government deliveries in 1971 and 17 percent in 1975, but in 1976 they moved up again, to 30 percent of government deliveries.[19]

The private side of arms sales remains significant, and there is good reason for the U.S. government to regulate strictly the commercial promotion of arms sales. The government itself should be the dominant actor in the U.S. arms trade.

Allowing U.S. firms a more active role and relegating the government to a licensing function would not depoliticize arms sales in sensitive cases: India would not be less unhappy over arms sales to Pakistan, or Israel over sales to Egypt, if the principal party was an American corporation rather than the U.S. government. And other countries are likely to see U.S. firms no less than government officials as instruments of U.S. policies and of U.S. "ruling circles." Putting arms sales in the hands of U.S. corporations, which are widely perceived as agents acting with the advice and consent of the U.S. government, hardly can render such transactions politically neutral in the eyes of foreign governments, though it

19. U.S. Department of Defense, Defense Security Assistance Agency, *Foreign Military Sales and Military Assistance Facts, December 1976* (DSAA, 1977), pp. 14 and 16; and DSAA, "Security Assistance Program, Volume 1, FY 1978," Congressional Presentation (DSAA, 1977; processed), p. 23.

could play down the appearance of a U.S. commitment to support governments merely because they purchase arms from the United States.

Pentagon sales officials, members of military assistance advisory groups, and embassy officers abroad, in the past at least, have been zealous in setting forth the merits and availability of U.S. arms to potential customers. Representatives of U.S. firms have been no less zealous. If the United States wishes to lessen foreign pressures to buy U.S. arms, it seems sensible not to whet foreign appetites. Strong controls placed on the sales activities of private arms agents are not unreasonable in this light. And if control and restraint are the emphasis in U.S. policy, it makes more sense to retain a central government role in military sales than to attempt to apply restraint through policy guidelines and licensing.

The positive reasons for the U.S. government role in arms sales are no less important. The Department of Defense is not only by far the largest purchaser of U.S. arms, it also finances most defense research and development and holds the patents on major weapons systems and their components. Moreover, it is responsible for the protection of sensitive technology. The scheduling of production and the delivery of equipment the Defense Department orders depends on government determination of the allocation and scheduling of deliveries to foreign buyers.

Most foreign governments see advantages in engaging the U.S. Department of Defense in their procurement planning and programs. In this way they obtain assurance of delivery, availability of spare parts, technical advice, and other assistance, plus the overall confidence provided by U.S. government undertakings. While some of these benefits could be provided as a supplement to commercial transactions, they come more naturally through government-to-government dealings.

More important, U.S. national interests in arms transactions may be subordinated or even perverted if the government role is a passive one. Where it seems wise to sell arms, the United States is concerned about the budgetary impact, about regional stability, and about the risks of U.S.–Soviet competition in the arming of neighboring states with different types of weapons among those that might be offered. These considerations can occupy the central place in decisions regarding sales only if the government plays the principal role in the transaction.

CHAPTER FOUR

Export of Arms Production Capabilities

Most nations have almost no arms industry and consequently must buy their weapons from one of the nine countries that control the great bulk of the arms trade. For a variety of reasons many of them are interested in starting a defense industry. Doing so is difficult, however. A broad industrial base and help from more advanced nations are indispensable. Even with these, a sharp spur—such as the virtual international isolation of Israel, Taiwan, or South Africa—may be required if the necessary sustained and focused effort is to be mounted.

Despite the difficulties and the examples of limited success, many countries continue to take an interest in defense production as they advance in industrialization, or seek to reduce the burden of arms imports on their foreign-exchange balance, or attempt to reduce their military, political, or economic dependence. With greater industrialization, more countries will become capable of producing arms. The proliferation of weapons manufacturers poses problems. Although the international arms trade may shrink as client states begin to produce their own weapons, the international tensions and conflicts, and ambitions and consequent military buildups of which the arms trade is a symptom, will not disappear. And as new arms producers yield to pressures to become arms suppliers, arms traffic and efforts to control and moderate it will become more complicated. As more countries become able to equip their forces and supply and maintain their operations, local conflicts may become less costly for the combatants to sustain, and containing and ending them may become more difficult for the international community.

The United States has long included in its transfers of defense articles and services—whether as assistance or as sales—weapons components, maintenance and production gear, and technology or technical advice and assistance to be used in local production of arms. Such transfers have gone primarily to NATO, Australia, Israel, Japan, and a number of other Asian countries that share U.S. defense objectives. They have been used not only to bolster common defense efforts but to reduce the military and economic burden on the United States.

The vehicles for carrying out cooperative ventures range from patents, blueprints, and industrial processes, manufacturing facilities and equipment, and technical advice and managerial know-how to joint production or development of weapons with one or several countries. Even in transfers of arms and military equipment, important information is inevitably provided. The items themselves, and the operating and maintenance manuals accompanying them, reveal something of their design and specifications and operating characteristics. That information can be useful to any country (friendly or hostile) interested in duplicating the item, in producing similar equipment requiring solution of some of the same technical problems, or in defending against the weapon. Consequently, items whose design or performance characteristics must be protected are classified, and any state that receives such items is required to protect the equipment and information pertaining to it.

Transfers of information or equipment that are made for the explicit purpose of adding to another country's capability to maintain, repair, modify, assemble, design, or produce arms and military equipment and components thereof are referred to by American officials as coproduction assistance. Both government sales and commercial sales licensed by the government can be used in these programs to provide know-how to foreign governments, international organizations, or designated foreign commercial producers. "The 'know-how' furnished through co-production programs may include research, development production data and/or manufacturing machinery or tools, raw or finished materiel, components or major sub-assemblies, managerial skills, procurement assistance or quality-control procedures."[1]

Over the long term, equipment or information supplied by the United States and used in licensed or joint production in other countries has a potential for more extensive conventional arms proliferation and greater attrition of U.S. control than do U.S. sales of weapons themselves. Thus

1. U.S. Department of Defense, *Military Assistance and Sales Manual* (GPO, 1974), pt. 3, chap. D, pp. 10–11.

legislative requirements for control over use of U.S. arms and their transfer to third parties should unequivocally apply to the output of licensed production abroad using U.S. know-how, technology, machinery, or components.

Congress, though, ended its statement of policy in the Foreign Assistance Act of 1961 with a reaffirmation of its support for political, military, and economic cooperation among the members of NATO. It urged that "multilateral programs of coordinated procurement, research, development, and production of defense articles . . . be expanded to the fullest extent possible to further the defense of the North Atlantic area."[2] And in 1968, noting that "it is increasingly difficult and uneconomic for any country, particularly a developing country, to fill all of its legitimate defense requirements from its own design and production base," the Foreign Military Sales Act extended U.S. cooperation to "those friendly countries to which it is allied by mutual defense treaties." The act confirmed that

it remains the policy of the United States to facilitate the common defense by entering into international arrangements with friendly countries which further the objective of applying agreed resources of each country to programs and projects of cooperative exchange of data, research, development, production, procurement, and logistics support to achieve specific national defense requirements and objectives of mutual concern.[3]

In May 1977 President Carter in his statement of U.S. arms transfer policy moved away from that position. "Coproduction agreements for significant weapons, equipment, and major components (beyond assembly of subcomponents and the fabrication of high-turnover spare parts) are prohibited," he said. "A limited class of items will be considered for coproduction arrangements, but with restrictions on third-country exports, since these arrangements are intended primarily for the coproducer's requirement."[4]

2. 75 Stat. 435.

3. 82 Stat. 1321. An amendment in 1972 to the Foreign Assistance Act specifies that no coproduction or licensed production that involves government credits or guarantees shall be approved until the secretary of state has given appropriate organs of Congress a full report, including "the probable impact of the proposed transaction on employment and production within the United States" (86 Stat. 33).

4. "Conventional Arms Transfer Policy: Statement by the President, May 19, 1977," *Weekly Compilation of Presidential Documents*, vol. 13 (May 23, 1977), p. 756.

Although the restrictions do not apply to nations with which the United States has "major defense treaties," coproduction agreements are likely to be less attractive to allies who wish not only to satisfy their own defense needs but also to produce arms for export.

Joint Production in NATO

Over the past thirty years the Western European allies of the United States have moved from almost complete dependence on U.S. military technology and weapons to a mixture of cooperation, coordination, and competition with the United States in military production.[5] Not only the United States and the European members of NATO but NATO itself as a planning and consultative organ have helped to identify and highlight common interests and ways of reconciling divergent national interests. The recent trend toward cooperation among European states and firms is part of the broader drive toward European political and economic integration, but it is also a protective reaction to fears of U.S. dominance of military technology.

After World War II, when reconstruction of basic industries and supporting facilities for industry and indeed for all aspects of society was of prime importance in Europe, the United States supplied most of its allies' arms through grant military assistance. In this period also almost $40 billion was invested in privately owned plants for manufacture of arms and other military goods in the United States, and another $15 billion in government-owned facilities. The purpose was to establish an industrial mobilization base for U.S. armed forces and NATO allies. U.S. policy, both statutory and executive, has consistently been to maintain a full range of U.S. research, development, and production capabilities, to avoid reliance on foreign sources of supply for any significant item, and to procure weapons from other countries only when there are overriding military and political advantages. This basically autarkic element of U.S. policy, often overlooked, has been a key factor in U.S.-NATO relations.

5. U.S. military technology has been no less central in the rebuilding of Japan's defense industries, and ties between Japanese and U.S. firms are close today. The complexities and problems have been less numerous, however, because of Japan's limited defense policy and military needs, its lack of interest in supplying arms to other countries, and its minimal demands on the United States for coordination and joint planning as compared with NATO's integrated staff and national components.

As European economic and industrial recovery progressed, arms assembly, design, and production resumed in Europe. Much—but not all—of the technology was initially American. The emphasis increasingly shifted from U.S. assistance to cooperative, coordinated, or joint efforts within the framework of NATO military and logistics planning and consultation. The first arrangements that the United States worked out to help NATO allies were cost-sharing agreements, under which material procured either in Europe or in the United States was paid for in part by grant military assistance and in part by the recipient nation. Shipbuilding in Norway was supported in this way, for example. Later, mutual weapons development agreements for research and development in advanced weapons systems were concluded with Belgium, France, Italy, Norway, the Netherlands, and the United Kingdom; they lapsed in the 1960s when military assistance to these nations was terminated.

Beginning in 1954 the United States furnished equipment and technical assistance to NATO allies through facilities assistance agreements to help them expand defense production; recipients agreed to make products available to other NATO nations at reasonable prices. The latter agreements were eventually succeeded by weapons production agreements, under the aegis of NATO. Joint production agreements covered the manufacture in Europe of some dozen systems, including missiles, aircraft, and detection and ground-control equipment for air defense.[6]

The cooperative ventures succeeded admirably in reducing exchange costs for the European countries, enabling them to buy weapons they could not have afforded otherwise. In some instances the final cost was lower than that in the United States, but in most cases it was somewhat higher; the cost, however, was in local currencies of the participants. The transfer of technology pushed European participants ahead by a decade or more. In addition, they learned how to manage complex systems, and they obtained sophisticated weapons. Several of them used the weapons simultaneously, widening standardization and consequently reducing some of the maintenance costs. But the projects were not wholly successful in stimulating wider industrial integration in Europe.[7]

Arms procurement within NATO became increasingly competitive, with national governments preferring arms of local design and manufacture where these satisfied military requirements. And in the 1960s several

6. Jack N. Behrman, *Multilateral Production Consortia: Lessons from NATO Experience,* a report prepared under contract to the Department of State, publication 8593 (GPO, 1971).

7. Ibid., p. 3.

NATO countries (the United Kingdom and France particularly) began to compete with the United States in arms markets around the world as well as within NATO. In its moves to capture a larger share of the European market, France has operated unilaterally where possible, but has turned to joint ventures with other European nations when necessary to match the United States in head-to-head competition. The United Kingdom, West Germany, and France have worked together on certain types of weapons systems in order not to be completely dependent on the United States. They and other Western European nations have concentrated their joint efforts in development and production of aircraft, aircraft engines, missiles, artillery, and electronics.

The array of weapons development and production programs that has sprung up has posed serious problems for NATO military planners. Today there is little compatibility in NATO's military equipment. For example, the United States, West Germany, France, and the United Kingdom have each developed a distinctive version of the main battle tank. By 1975 the NATO missile inventory included thirteen varieties of close-range, antitank weapons, six different short-range missiles, seven versions of medium-range missiles, and five separate long-range missile systems. One of NATO's tactical air forces had eleven different types of combat aircraft and three, incompatible systems for command and control.[8]

The operational and logistic penalties of such a hodge-podge of equipment, and the waste of valuable technical resources devoted to its development are obvious. A more rational pattern of NATO weapons development and production would require standardization of equipment and specialization in production. Interested members could either manufacture and sell systems of special merit or share in development and production projects or in the manufacture and assembly of components of major systems (as the European consortium members in the sales agreement for F-16 aircraft are doing).

The United States is not hostile to such arrangements. The Department of Defense has shown its willingness—at times somewhat tentative—to purchase European products, despite congressional reservations, and to negotiate contractual arrangements under which European weap-

8. Thomas A. Callaghan, Jr., *U.S.-European Economic Cooperation in Military and Civil Technology*, rev. ed. (Center for Strategic and International Studies, Georgetown University, 1975), p. 21.

ons systems are fabricated in the United States. The U.S. Marine Corps, for example, has invested in the British Harrier, an aircraft that can take off and land vertically.[9]

In 1975 Secretary Schlesinger approved a major procurement policy change, allowing greater use of European-designed weapons systems. The Army shortly thereafter awarded a contract to the Hughes Aircraft Company for "advanced development" of the Roland II, a missile system developed by a consortium of German and French companies that control its production.[10] The secretary of defense in selecting the Roland II was, for all intents and purposes, rejecting an American missile, the Chaparral—an action that seemed likely to spur Roland sales in other countries at the expense of its American competitor. Similarly, in 1976 the Defense Department decided to purchase Belgian-made machine guns rather than an American-made competitor for use in U.S. tanks. When the U.S. Army chose a new American tank, the XM-1, over a West German competitor, it directed the manufacturer to design it to accommodate the 120 mm gun of the German tank, which, in turn, was to accommodate the turbine engine used in the XM-1.[11] In addition to major logistical advantages, such weapons standardization is likely to produce savings in costs.

In recent years Congress too has become interested in coordinated development of NATO weapons. The 1977 act authorizing the Department of Defense appropriation gave particular encouragement to coproduction agreements:

It is the sense of the Congress that progress toward the realization of the objectives of standardization and interoperability would be enhanced by expanded inter-Allied procurement of arms and equipment within the North Atlantic Treaty Organization. . . . Expanded inter-Allied procurement would be facilitated by greater reliance on licensing and coproduction agreements among the signatories of the North Atlantic Treaty.[12]

The effort to standardize and make the best possible use of alliance technical and industrial resources involves a complex balance of national interests. Each NATO nation must find ways of maintaining its indus-

9. Department of Defense, "Annual Department of Defense Report, FY 1975" (1974; processed), p. 145.

10. Callaghan, U.S.-*European Economic Cooperation*, pp. 52–53.

11. In 1978 the army decided to purchase the German gun after having placed an earlier order for an American manufactured gun. *New York Times*, Feb. 1, 1978.

12. 90 Stat. 931.

trial and other popular support for its defense budget and of avoiding a dependent or inferior role in NATO affairs. For the United States, standardization and coproduction can no longer mean a one-way flow. Secretary of Defense Harold Brown in March 1977 declared the United States' determination to "achieve greater commonality and more of a two-way street."[13]

Cooperation with the Developing Countries

Cooperation or assistance in arms production abroad presents quite different practical and political problems for the United States when developing countries are involved. In military technology and the arms industry, as in industrialization generally, these countries need different kinds of help at different stages. From importing machinery or manufactured goods, they look successively to building up the capacity to maintain and repair imported goods, then to building spare parts, then to assembling finished goods using some locally produced components, then to producing and assembling all but the most intricate components, then to developing their own modified or new designs.[14]

Few countries reach the ultimate stage of self-sufficiency in the arms industry. Only a handful of advanced industrial states develop and produce high-performance military aircraft, for example, and only a few more manufacture their own design of simpler military aircraft. The story is the same for tanks, artillery, missiles, naval vessels. In India, Brazil, and Argentina, there have been partial successes and many abortive efforts in production of weapons, even when designs and components have been imported and foreign technical help has been available. Israel and South Africa, with a good industrial and technical base and the spur of political isolation and formal or de facto embargo by most arms suppliers, have had some success in local production of weapons, and even in developing new models, though with substantial technical help from abroad. Most developing countries—even those with some progress in industrialization—have not moved beyond the operation of repair, over-

13. *NATO Posture and Initiatives*, Hearing before the Senate Armed Services Committee, 95:1 (GPO, 1977), p. 10.

14. For an excellent discussion of the process as it relates to arms, see Stockholm International Peace Research Institute (SIPRI), *Arms Trade with the Third World* (Stockholm: Almquist and Winksell, 1971), pp. 723–92.

haul, and modification facilities for imported equipment and the assembly and manufacture of parts for small arms and simple equipment.

The obstacles to further development are formidable, for "a whole range of back-up industries, adequate infrastructure, skilled personnel and so on" is necessary for the production of sophisticated weapons.[15] "For a country with an underdeveloped economy . . . the most usual obstacles are the shortage of local raw material (for example, finished steel, aluminum or titanium) or unexpected rises in production costs."[16]

A high degree of proficiency in engineering, management, and quality control obviously is demanded in a jet aircraft that has hundreds of thousands of parts, or advanced surface-to-air missiles that involve thousands of components and spares. Few nations can attempt production of such items, but many may be able to undertake the maintenance, overhaul, and manufacture of spare parts. Whether a success or a failure, such ventures, even when foreign help is available, are likely to prove expensive for developing countries. Initial investment costs are high, as are the costs of learning and breaking in production processes, the costs of components procured abroad (usually disproportionately more expensive than complete equipment), and the unit costs of items produced in small runs (as opposed to the unit costs of producers with large local and export markets). That countries persist in efforts at setting up indigenous arms production is evidence of the strength of the driving motives: national pride and prestige, and the related desire to escape from client status; or a need to be self-reliant in facing hostility and military threats, coupled with political isolation and even embargo (Israel, Taiwan, South Africa, India, Egypt). There is an incentive to sell the arms that are produced to third countries to recoup some of the investment and if possible to lower unit costs by increasing production; and politically, achieving the status of an arms supplier is a way of acquiring ties and cooperative relations with other nations.

The only deliberate efforts the United States has made to transfer weapons technology to developing countries have been to build up local maintenance and repair capabilities. Because the creation of defense industries demands a considerable range of human and material capacities, the United States has been loath to disseminate its skills to developing countries. It has preferred that the resources an arms industry would re-

15. SIPRI, *World Armaments and Disarmament, SIPRI Yearbook 1973* (Stockholm: Almquist and Winksell, 1973), p. 350.
16. Ibid.

quire be directed toward economic development, and has used military aid to satisfy these countries' needs for defense equipment.

Most of the countries that have received U.S. military aid have attempted to acquire production know-how in a handful of fairly basic fields. The starting point, almost invariably, has been in the manufacture of small-arms ammunition; in some instances this has been followed by the production of grenades, launchers, and artillery shells. In Asia, there has been a surge in the construction of rifle production facilities:[17] in the Philippines, South Korea, and Singapore, agreements with the Colt Arms Company to permit manufacture of the M-16 rifle (for domestic use only); in Malaysia a joint venture with Swiss and West German firms to manufacture an automatic rifle used by NATO forces; and in Thailand an agreement with a West German firm to fabricate a rifle comparable to the M-16. In addition, Taiwan and South Korea assemble U.S. helicopters and ground forces vehicles; both are aggressively working to become self-sufficient in a growing number of weapons fields.

In the Middle East the only substantial productive capacity is located in Israel. Israel's emphasis has been on improvement of other countries' weapons systems rather than on indigenous design, development, and production of defense weapons. It has produced tanks and fighter aircraft that are hybrid systems based on imported designs.[18]

The Arab oil-producing states and Iran have concentrated on acquiring arms from major Western powers and the Soviet Union, but past hesitation of Western suppliers and political pressure by the Soviet Union have encouraged them to plan for indigenous assembly and production of armaments. In 1975 Arab oil-producing nations agreed to support the establishment of a pan-Arab arms industry—the Arab States Military Industrial Organization.[19] The center of this effort was to be in Egypt, the only member country with trained personnel and skilled labor. The group's first major effort, backed by more than $1 billion in capital, was to be directed at production of advanced aircraft; designs and technical know-how were expected to come from Britain and France.[20]

Pakistan which has strong religious ties to the Arab world is also a possible source of assistance to the new effort; it is strengthening political

17. *Washington Post*, Apr. 14, 1974.
18. The *Kfir*, for example, is a hybrid design.
19. *New York Times*, May 14, 1975.
20. *Strategic Survey 1976* (International Institute for Strategic Studies, 1977), p. 23.

ties with its Arab neighbors by posting administrators, technicians, military advisors, and air force pilots throughout the Middle East, and especially along the Arab side of the Persian Gulf. Pakistan has manpower and some technical skill as well as experience in operating a variety of weapons systems. Its defense production already includes warships, aircraft, and missiles.[21]

In Iran, establishment of a defense industry has received almost as much official emphasis as direct purchases of arms. Iran has concentrated on the manufacture of subsystems and components, the establishment of jointly owned operations and maintenance facilities, and some joint production of weapons. Most of its cooperative ventures are with the U.S. government and defense industry. Iran's major aircraft industry, located near Tehran, is jointly owned by Iranian interests (51 percent) and the Northrop Corporation (49 percent). It provides operations and virtually all maintenance services for the Iranian armed forces, including maintenance of sophisticated U.S. aircraft. Another U.S. company, Bell Helicopter, has licensed production of various subsystems and airframe components for helicopters in Iran, and the Iranian government now owns a helicopter operations and maintenance facility that was established jointly with an Italian firm.[22]

Iran has also begun to develop an electronics industry with the participation of U.S. and British firms. The Hughes aerospace firm contracted with the Iranian government in 1974 to construct a plant for missile-guidance systems; initially it would be used for maintenance and training purposes but eventually to fabricate complete components, subsystems, and systems.[23] British and U.S. electronics firms have also been reported to be cooperating in setting up a communications facility.[24]

In Africa, the only country that is attempting to produce arms on a large scale is South Africa; the United States, in conformance with the UN embargo, refrains from cooperation or sales there. The United States also embargoed arms sales to India and Pakistan until 1975. India has been developing a broad armaments industry with substantial technical

21. Ibid., p. 22; and Robert Hotz, "Export Boom Continues," *Aviation Week and Space Technology*, July 8, 1974, p. 7.

22. *Aviation Week and Space Technology*, Sept. 9, 1974, p. 13.

23. Ibid., Apr. 22, 1974, p. 23; and *International Defense Review*, vol. 7 (August 1974), p. 469.

24. "Military Aspects of Communication '74'," *International Defense Review*, vol. 7 (August 1974), p. 527.

assistance from the Soviet Union and Western European nations. Latin American countries (Brazil and Argentina) tend to look to Western Europe for technology and advice, partly for historical reasons and partly to avoid dependence on the United States.

A Policy Governing Joint Production

Developing the capacity to produce major weapons is a difficult, costly, and lengthy process—particularly if complicated components such as aircraft engines and electronic gear are not procured abroad. Yet in a number of countries—Brazil, Argentina, Egypt, Iran, Greece, Turkey, Spain, India, South Korea, and Taiwan—the broader economic and industrial transformation that is now under way may make feasible, in the decade ahead, technical goals that were only recently unattainable. And for other less developed countries, defense production facilities that the United States has helped to set up may be the first steps toward self-sufficiency.

The practical application of President Carter's intention to prohibit coproduction agreements for significant equipment will be to discourage and withhold support from ten or a score of new industrial nations that would like to become self-sufficient in production of arms and military equipment—and also sources of arms supplies for other countries. Industrializing states, of course, will often be able to decide their own priorities and exercise them. The constraints that limited investment funds and foreign exchange impose on some countries, for instance, will seldom inhibit the Persian Gulf states. And major arms-producing nations in Europe may enter into licensed or joint-production ventures with developing states to increase their share of the market or gain a politically valued role.

The United States must be sure that what it does in response to requests for production expertise represents balanced and deliberate choices among a variety of possible actions. Definition and statement of U.S. policy, including congressional consultation, hearings, and (if necessary) legislation, might prevent events and short-term interests from involving the United States in another nation's military buildup before the implications of these actions are realized. Policy is likely to have to be formulated in regional terms, for incentives and economic and technical capabilities vary sharply among the Middle East (where the need for a policy is most urgent), Asia, and Latin America—and U.S. interests there vary also.

On those coproduction agreements that are allowed to go forward, the United States should restrict production to assure that arms produced abroad are not more freely available than those produced at home. Individual decisions on export of weapons technology will have to be taken with great caution and care, with reference to both near-term and longer-term consequences. Measures to assure individual consideration may indeed be the heart of sound policy, since general guidelines, even relating to major regions, may be difficult to formulate or carry out; most decisions will probably have to be unique and ad hoc.

Export of U.S. weapons technology has limited intrinsic value for the United States and will at best be second choice to sales of finished arms and military equipment. By the tests of efficiency, economics, and control, sales are the preferable method of transferring arms: they provide needed weapons more quickly, at lower cost, and with greater reliability; the return to the U.S. economy is greater; and control and safeguards are more clearly defined and surer. They are also preferable from broader perspectives of international development, stability, and peace: proliferation of arms producers absorbs capital and skilled management and labor, is likely to raise the cost and lower the reliability of equipment, and complicates the tasks of restraining conventional arms buildups and transfers and of moderating regional strains and rivalries. And when hostility to neighbors or ambition for status or regional hegemony is the motive for independent arms production, international order and tranquility are likely to suffer.

With the spread of industrialization, the capacity to produce military equipment will grow. The Organization of Petroleum Exporting Countries has declared that "the transfer of technology ... constitutes a major test of adherence of the developed countries to the principle of international cooperation in favour of development."[25] The "products of a high technological content" that they expect to be enabled to produce would certainly include modern arms. Thus the United States will face demands for transfers of weapons technology as a condition for political or military cooperation or of arms purchases. Competition will be evident from the Soviet Union on occasion, as well as Britain and France. Hard

25. "Solemn Declaration of the Conference of the Sovereigns and Heads of States of the OPEC Member Countries," Algiers, Mar. 4–6, 1975.

choices will be faced, where either rejection or acceptance will be unattractive.

The immediate availability of U.S. military equipment and spare parts can in some instances counter impulses to embark on local production, with its costs and delays and uncertainties. Some local activities, however, make sense—repair, maintenance, minor modification of weapons produced in the United States—and they do not involve the United States so closely in another country's military establishment as provision of U.S. services might. Technology and equipment for such activities are not sensitive.

In sales of major equipment like the F-16 fighter aircraft to the European consortium, local assembly and production of components may be required conditions of the purchase. If the conditions are acceptable, such sales may offer a net economic advantage to the United States and no diminution of control.

Licensed or joint production also may be the only way the United States can keep another country from turning to local production or purchasing arms from a third country. Again, the economic balance from license fees and services and components may be favorable. In addition to contractual stipulations regarding security, end use, and sales to third parties, practical U.S. control may be facilitated if such key sophisticated components as jet engines or electronic gear are manufactured in the United States.

Production licenses should stipulate the territory, if any, in which sales to third countries will be permitted or considered, but such sales should not be necessary to make the licensees' production viable. The United States does not want its customers' impulse to seek sales to counter the U.S. objective of moderating the arms trade and discouraging aggressive sales, nor from a commercial point of view does it want to set up competitors for U.S. manufacturers.

The provisions of the Arms Export Control Act governing security protection, retransfer, and use of arms and military equipment, and ineligibility in case of violation, should be specifically applied to items produced abroad under license from the United States or dependent on U.S. know-how, manufacturing equipment, or major components. If, for example, U.S. tanks or aircraft are manufactured or assembled abroad, any third country that buys them from the licensee must be required to accept the conditions regarding security protection, retransfer, and use that would apply to a direct sale by the United States. As a practical matter, there will probably have to be a limit beyond which U.S. control will not apply.

Proposals to transfer weapons technology, license foreign production, and produce arms abroad should be reviewed with deliberation. They should be authorized only if they are in the national interest, and their scope and limiting conditions should be precisely defined. U.S. commercial and broad political interests coincide in this respect.

Such a reserved approach to foreign production will encounter impatience and threats to turn elsewhere. If, however, the United States meets reasonable requests for arms purchases and is willing to engage in limited transfers of technology or cooperative production, it will be able to tolerate the political costs of refusing to help establish fully independent production in other countries. The rejected applicant may of course attempt to set up production on its own or turn to other outside help. In most indigenous ventures the process will prove uncertain and lengthy, and U.S. refusal to help will thus have some salutary delaying effect. If the project appears economically and technically unsound, the venturing country will have to bear the risk and costs of going ahead. If it points toward the proliferation of conventional arms, the difficulty and delay and uncertainty of the unaided project will in themselves be a reasonable return for U.S. abstention.

CHAPTER FIVE

Application of Arms Policy

Conclusions about how the transfer of U.S. arms and military technology should be controlled must eventually be applied to specific situations. In some cases deciding whether a particular country may receive arms, of what types and amounts, and by what means is relatively easy. In many instances, however, highly arguable judgments must be made.

The United States, it is generally agreed, has a major interest in the security and stability of Western Europe and in cooperating with nations there. Similarly, it is interested in the security of Japan and in maintaining an association with Japan that will enable it to remain a lightly armed, nonnuclear power; large-scale Japanese rearmament, particularly with nuclear arms, would be profoundly destabilizing in Asia. Elsewhere, U.S. security interests are generally recognized to be limited: There is a special interest in preventing hostile external powers from establishing bases and forces in the Caribbean and in maintaining unhindered use of the Panama Canal. American support of Israel is long-standing and continuing. The United States is committed historically and by treaty to the defense of South Korea, a commitment aimed at assuring stability in the region that many Japanese regard as important to the security of their country. Similar commitments have been made to the Philippines, Australia, New Zealand, and Taiwan.

Where U.S. security interests are defined by treaty, and U.S. allies are able to pay for the weapons they need, dilemmas of policy seldom arise. But when alliance partners are dependent on some aid, the terms of exchange are likely to include intangible interests that are matters of debate within the United States. When assistance is given in pursuit of U.S. security goals yet outside the bounds of treaty commitments, arms trans-

69

fers are often volatile issues. Some of the largest sales of U.S. arms are now being made to states in the Middle East, and a number of those states are pressing for joint or licensed production of U.S. weapons. The decisions that are made there clearly must apply to the transfer of technology as well as arms. This chapter examines the history and prospects of major recipients of U.S. arms and the possibility of regulating arms sales through international agencies.

Treaty Partners

The major overseas security interests of the United States closely match its treaty commitments. The United States has no formal tie, however, with Israel, to which it gives major help. At the other extreme, Pakistan, a partner in the Southeast Asia collective defense treaty, receives no U.S. support for its major preoccupation, its rivalry with India. The NATO allies, except for Portugal and Turkey, and Japan, Australia, New Zealand, and Taiwan can easily fund their own defense programs. And the countries of Latin America, as well as the Philippines and Thailand, while less prosperous, are able to deal with their less demanding external security problems. Only South Korea, among U.S. allies, faces an actively hostile neighbor and is not fully able to fund its own defense. Thus it still receives substantial U.S. military assistance. Aid continues to be offered to a few other allies—notably in southern Europe—but principally as a means of gaining base rights in those countries.

Industrial Allies

Most of the United States' NATO allies, Japan, Australia, and New Zealand do not need, and do not receive, security assistance, and their military purchases from the United States do not raise novel policy issues. Common security interests are defined by treaty; these allies can make their own assessment of their financial ability to buy and of their security perils and arms requirements (independently and in consultation with the United States), and they are able to bargain effectively on prices and coproduction arrangements. With partners thus able to hold their own, even aggressive U.S. salesmanship, at times, of major weapon systems is acceptable practice.

The United States has devoted a good deal of effort to persuading its

NATO allies to assume a larger and fairer share of the common defense burden, and at times has sought to ease the burden of overseas deployments or the U.S. balance of payments by urging arms purchases by its allies. A single-minded effort to monopolize the alliance market or undercut competition by offering inferior equipment to alliance partners would work against the basic objective of increasing allied nations' defense contributions. European taxpayers and treasury ministers cannot be expected to keep up defense budgets if no major arms purchases are made from local firms. Hence U.S. readiness—as in the sale of F-16 aircraft to NATO—to make arrangements for a sizable amount of local assembly and manufacture of components. The United States also refrains from using its massive arms development and production base to preempt even more of the NATO market because it recognizes the need to exploit fully the technical and industrial capabilities of the alliance.

Those problems that do arise in relation to U.S. sales to major allies —and they can be complex and contentious—do not seriously threaten U.S. or international security and stability. They are matters of commercial friction, optimization of efforts and results, and accommodation of political and economic interests—the kinds of problems that can be worked out in bilateral and multilateral discussion and bargaining among political equals with shared security interests.

Perhaps the thorniest issue in the future will relate to NATO countries' interest in selling to other nations the arms they manufacture under coproduction agreements. Although West Germany has refrained from large-scale arms exports to countries that are not allies of the United States, Britain and France have not. They and other NATO nations will probably need to export jointly produced arms to lower unit costs of production and to support their trade balances. If the United States refuses to allow sales to third countries, the competitive advantage of European arms produced in cooperation with U.S. corporations may disappear altogether. Should U.S. firms find it attractive in the future to join with European corporations in the development of advanced armaments, the United States will feel even greater pressure to allow sales to third countries. In this contest of principles, NATO standardization and a policy of restraining the arms trade will clash head-on.

United States willingness to purchase for U.S. armed forces European-designed weapons systems rather than U.S.-developed products—and thereby accept NATO standardization as a two-way street—will almost certainly mean an absence of control over the sale of these arms to non-

NATO nations. These weapons would be all the more desirable to third countries if no U.S. competitor existed and if they were marked as having been bought by a superpower.

The Southern Corners of Europe

Greece, Turkey, Spain, and Portugal are treaty partners of the United States that have received substantial amounts of U.S. military aid and continue to be of interest because of assets they can offer in return. All four are buying an increasing portion of their arms, but assistance continues to be given in exchange for rights the United States believes are important. That aid has been a matter of issue with these allies.

Turkey's seizure of a substantial portion of Cyprus in 1974 and illegal use of equipment given in exchange for U.S. access to bases in Turkey has created major disagreement over the transfer of arms to both Turkey and Greece. The policy debate in the United States has raged around the Cyprus dispute. This dispute will not be easily resolved, but the parties involved (Greece, Turkey, and Greek and Turkish Cypriots) and their European allies may contribute more to a settlement than the United States can. Unfortunately, the 1975 U.S. embargo on arms transfers to Turkey and its later relaxation were widely seen as leverage to bring about a Cyprus settlement. But the principle at issue was adherence to the agreement restricting use of American arms. Strict adherence is unlikely in an untidy world; flat defiance by a recipient and ally is not tolerable, however. The protestations that the embargo should be ended because of the security importance of Turkish bases overlook the importance of the bases in Greece—particularly those in Crete used by the U.S. Sixth Fleet and by NATO forces for training and operational readiness.

The essential condition for easing or lifting the embargo must be reconfirmation of the agreement that arms provided by the United States shall not be used in conflicts between U.S. allies or other friendly states. Good relations between Greece and Turkey—difficult enough to attain—and reestablishment of good relations between them and the United States will be shaky or impossible on any other basis. And such good relations are probably more important to NATO and local security than is the flow of U.S. arms to Greek and Turkish forces so long as the NATO and U.S. security umbrellas remain.

Security assistance is asked to do more than it can in the 1976 U.S.

accords with Turkey (committing $1 billion in aid over four years)[1] and Greece (providing for $700 million in aid over four years).[2] Priorities appear curiously askew. Aid is used overtly to pay allies for bases and facilities for the common defense. Greater concern is given to retention of U.S. facilities and to maintenance of arms and aid flows than to the restoration of Greek-Turkish relations.

Objections by Greece to the resumption of arms flows to Turkey, and similar reactions in Congress, could portend collapse of the accord with Turkey and heightened U.S.–Turkish tension. By its exposure in the controversy, the United States has made itself the scapegoat for continued stalemate in Cyprus negotiations. And the value the United States obviously places on bases will not be lost on the Greeks and Turks when they look in the future for leverage to gain either political support or security aid.

An alternative to continuing aid to Greece and Turkey would be to complete any deliveries now agreed to, provide credit for sale of equipment for NATO-oriented modernization programs that strain local financing capabilities, and continue cash sales with a formal reiteration of the mutual-security purposes of all arms transfers and the U.S. right to suspend deliveries in the event of use of U.S. arms for other purposes.

The mutual-security commitments between Greece and Turkey, and with the United States, are valuable and should continue. The main assurance of their security is U.S. and NATO backing under the NATO treaty. They should, in like manner, make their fair contribution to the common defense effort (including base facilities for NATO and U.S. use). East–West relations are such that there is not a strong case for U.S. aid in providing arms to deter or repel an attack by the Warsaw Pact. Despite problems of high oil payments and economic slowdown, the Greek economy is increasingly sound, and Turkey is making development progress. Thus, ending military grants need not be a significant blow to the military posture of the alliance.

If a gesture of U.S. support and solidarity is called for beyond credit sales, economic aid or military supporting assistance would avoid putting the United States in the middle of Greek–Turk military confrontation. In addition to aiding economic growth, it would help to build the economic base of their defense effort, which is perhaps of more long-term significance for the NATO–Warsaw Pact balance than more military hardware

1. *Department of State Bulletin*, Apr. 19, 1976, p. 532.
2. *New York Times*, Apr. 18, 1976.

now. Continued credit sales of equipment related to NATO plans would be justified support of security; they would also help the Turks politically as well as financially in their adjustment from transfers by grant to purchases.

The direct case for security assistance to Portugal and Spain also rests on the U.S. need for bases. In these countries, complex internal political matters complicate the calculation of a reasonable and acceptable quid pro quo for base rights.

Portugal, a member of NATO, was until recently preoccupied with defense of its African empire, rather than its collective defense role in NATO. This preoccupation posed a political problem for the United States; thus security assistance was predicated on the use of U.S. arms only for NATO obligations, and only small amounts of supplies were provided. This quid pro quo for U.S. access to facilities in the Azores, particularly the use of Lajes airfield, was acceptable to Portugal, especially because the United States also stood by Portugal against the most extreme UN resolutions and other political moves. Since the end of the colonial empire and the installation of a new regime, modest security assistance (as well as economic assistance) has continued to have at least as much symbolic as practical significance to the Portuguese government in its efforts to retain its place in NATO and its ties with the United States during a turbulent transition period.

The Spanish government, by contrast, has made an effort to obtain not only arms and other security aid from the United States, but security commitments and political support. At a time when the Franco regime was generally isolated in Western Europe, Spanish negotiators were successful in getting substantial security assistance—over $200 million in the first half of the 1970s[3]—as well as defense cooperation (short of a formal treaty) and conspicuous political ties and support in return for military bases.

After the death of Franco the United States and Spain signed a treaty of friendship and cooperation and supplemental arrangements[4] providing $1.22 billion in military and economic benefits to Spain over a five-year period. The substantial military aid ($735 million) is intended to

3. U.S. Agency for International Development, *U.S. Overseas Loans and Grants and Assistance from International Organizations: Obligations and Authorizations, July 1, 1945–June 30, 1975* (AID, 1976), p. 158.
4. Details of the agreement are from *Department of State Bulletin,* Mar. 22, 1976, pp. 362–63.

demonstrate the practical advantages of the political change that is under way in Spain and to encourage support by the military of a monarchy moving toward Western constitutional and political processes. It serves also as rent for U.S. use of bases and facilities in Spain. The number of facilities available, and of the U.S. units using them, has been cut back but U.S. rights to their use and for overflights by aircraft in transit to third countries have been reconfirmed, although it is unclear whether the United States could exercise these rights in the event of a new Middle East war. Spain denied permission to use its bases and airspace during the 1973 Middle East war.

The United States also has agreed to withdraw its nuclear submarines and other equipment that the Spanish assert make their country a tempting target. The presidential letter transmitting the friendship treaty to the Senate states flatly that it "does not expand the existing United States defense commitment in the North Atlantic Treaty area nor does it create an additional bilateral one." It does have provisions "dealing with military planning and coordination, to help develop an active Spanish contribution to western security."[5] It includes plans for leasing and selling sophisticated aircraft to Spain.

If the political rationale for the treaty is accepted as valid during a sensitive transition period, the military assistance programs do not seem exorbitant. Over the longer term, however, such aid is questionable. Spain's security problems are mainly internal. There is no significant external threat. If Spain does move into association with or membership in NATO and become a formal ally, the need for special help (or for base rental) should be obviated. Even if it does not, it is relatively prosperous and not in need of grants or even sales credit indefinitely. Open-ended U.S. security assistance commitments are not easily justified. Increasingly, transfers ought to be by means of government sales that are not supported by credits or guarantees.

South Korea

Since the end of the Vietnam War, South Korea has been the only U.S. ally in Asia whose needs justified a large amount of security aid. South Korea presents perhaps the most complex case in the assistance program, because of the active threat from North Korea, past and current U.S. commitments, the interests of four major powers (the United States,

5. Ibid., p. 362.

the USSR, China, and Japan) in the Korean peninsula, U.S. troops stationed in South Korea, an authoritarian regime that is actively criticized in the United States and opposed in South Korea, and a vigorous economy dependent on external trade and vulnerable to world economic upheavals. The phasing out of military grants to South Korea that began in fiscal 1977 is related to broader and more crucial decisions on the U.S. security role in East Asia and the Pacific.

From the time that the hostilities between North and South Korea were brought to an end in 1953 until 1976, the United States provided about $13 billion in military and economic assistance to South Korea.[6] When the first withdrawal of U.S. troops was proposed in 1971, a modernization plan was worked out for the South Korean forces that called for $1.5 billion in U.S. military aid, sales on credit, and transfers of excess defense articles, including sizable quantities of armor, artillery, combat aircraft, and antiaircraft weapons.[7] Before the modernization plan was completed, the South Korean government in 1975 announced a new improvement program for its armed forces, with substantial purchases of arms from the U.S. government on both cash and credit bases.[8]

Unless the South Korean economy slides seriously, the key decision in ending the aid relationship is whether it might be an excessive shock, as U.S. ground forces are being withdrawn. Security assistance can be an important tool of a U.S. policy aimed at maintaining stability in the Korean peninsula. The military balance between North and South Korea and the reserve shown by China and the Soviet Union toward North Korean efforts for reunification by force are important blocks to renewed hostility between North and South. So is the viability of an independent South Korea.

But President Park Chung Hee's government has become increasingly authoritarian since he imposed a constitution on the South Korean electorate in 1972 that gave him absolute political power.[9] Violent protests against police repression and tightened controls over political dissent have captured international attention, and the Park regime's lack of regard for human rights caused Congress in 1974 to put a ceiling on

6. AID, *U.S. Loans and Grants, July 1, 1945–June 30, 1976*, p. 75.
7. *Foreign Assistance Act of 1972*, Hearings before the House Committee on Foreign Affairs, 92:2 (GPO, 1972), pt. 1, pp. 162–63.
8. *Washington Post*, Dec. 29, 1975.
9. *New York Times*, Nov. 22, 1972.

military aid to South Korea.[10] Accusations in 1976 and subsequent investigation of widespread campaign contributions to U.S. congressmen and senators by agents of the South Korean government have further strained U.S. relations with South Korea.

But the issue extends beyond distaste for U.S. association with a repressive and otherwise obnoxious regime. If security assistance is justified as a means of political leverage as well as reinforcement of military capabilities, then it should be used to help South Korea move toward a more representative, less explosively unstable political configuration.

Other Allies in Asia

Assistance can also be used politically in the Philippines. There is no external threat to Philippine security justifying U.S. military aid ($41 million in security assistance was proposed in fiscal 1978),[11] but U.S. defense policy and posture in Asia require the retention of U.S. bases in the Philippines. President Marcos's call for renegotiation of the security and base arrangements in parallel with his opening of relations with China and Vietnam puts a practical, political stamp on the Philippine side of negotiations. On the U.S. side, arrangements for continued use of bases cannot escape the pressure of precedent set in the aid-for-bases deals made in Europe in 1976. But U.S. negotiators should heed the 1976 act of Congress in setting the terms of military aid. The repressive measures taken under martial law to deal with insurgency in the Philippines are in sharp conflict with views on human rights that the new U.S. law governing arms transfers intends should influence any political use of U.S. aid.

A different political use of aid is possible in Taiwan. That economically flourishing country can easily supply its own defense needs as long as the threat of the People's Republic of China does not increase. In fiscal 1977 Taiwan purchased an estimated $235 million in arms from the United States and received credits estimated at $35 million. The 1978 proposal called for $225 million in sales including $25 million in credits.[12] Taiwan also has a developing arms industry, producing aircraft and mis-

10. 88 Stat. 1802.
11. U.S. Department of Defense, Defense Security Assistance Agency, "Security Assistance Program, Volume 1, FY 1978," Congressional Presentation (DSAA, 1977; processed), p. 4.
12. Ibid., p. 19.

siles among other things. The United States will want to continue to sell
arms to Taiwan and perhaps allow some coproduction there. In its delicate relations with the two Chinas, the United States might want to
continue some small amount of credits as a reassuring gesture to Taiwan.

In Thailand the main determinant of U.S. security assistance ended
with the end of hostilities in Indochina. The nature of future security aid,
like any U.S. military presence in Thailand, needs to be carefully related
to the Thai role in the regional political and military balance. In 1969,
during the Vietnam War, as many as 48,000 U.S. troops operated out of
93 installations in Thailand; by the end of 1976, the only U.S. military
were those attached to the U.S. embassy, a medical research laboratory,
and the joint U.S.–Thai military advisory group.[13]

Thailand and the United States remain partners in the SEATO
treaty.[14] Despite its demand that U.S. forces in Thailand be withdrawn
after the end of the Vietnam War, and that the SEATO organization be
dismantled, Thailand recognizes the treaty and expects the U.S. defense
commitment therein to remain in force. The United States is interested in
good relations with Thailand and in Thai freedom from external dominance. Thus the U.S. policy of "loosening alignments" is by no means
inconsistent with the adjustment Thailand is making to the new situation
in Southeast Asia. The Thai must take responsibility for shaping their
future relations with Vietnam and China, as well as resolving internal
power jockeyings between the military and civilians and handling the
local insurgency.

Neither a substantial nor a continuing program of aid to Thailand is
likely to be warranted. The insurgency is properly a responsibility of the
Thai government, and the key to dealing with it is shrewd tactics, proper
organization, and good political judgment. The Thai financial and
balance-of-payments situation is relatively favorable. Equipment needs
will not be massive and might increasingly be obtained by more politically neutral cash purchases. In any event, the United States should be
responsive to Thai concerns and policies and avoid using security or
other aid to maintain Thai dependence on the United States or identification with U.S. interests. If aid appears to be warranted, economic aid
may be a wiser response than military help.

Whether an announced policy of restraint in arms sales is a workable

13. *Keesings Contemporary Archives*, 22 (1976), p. 28101.
14. SEATO as an organization was terminated on June 30, 1977. The
treaty continues. *New York Times*, July 1, 1977.

attitude toward a treaty partner is being tested in Pakistan. In February 1975 the ten-year-old embargo on arms sales to Pakistan and India was lifted. The State Department announced that both countries were eligible to buy arms on a cash basis, but that no government credit would be available; arms deliveries were not to "affect the underlying strategic balance." The embargo, on all arms shipments except nonlethal items and spare parts and ammunition for previously furnished U.S. end items, had been designed to keep the United States out of a South Asian political and military rivalry and in a position to participate in development efforts in both countries.

It is not entirely clear why the policy was changed—anymore than it was clear why the United States tilted so perceptibly toward Pakistan at the time of the birth of Bangladesh. Secretary of State Kissinger's public rationale was specious:

> It seemed to us, however, that to maintain an embargo against a friendly country with which we have an allied relationship, while its neighbor was producing and acquiring nearly a billion dollars worth of arms a year, was morally, politically, and symbolically improper . . . it seemed to us an anomaly to embargo one country in the area, to be the only country in the world to be embargoing this country, when its neighbor was not exercising a comparable restraint.[15]

The U.S. embargo, however, was on the two countries, Pakistan and India. And the reference to an "allied relationship" is misleading, since SEATO is an anticommunist alliance and Pakistan makes no secret that its procurement planning is related to India. Moreover, Kissinger did not claim that Pakistan was imperiled or that U.S. arms were needed for its security. In fact, he stated that other countries do not embargo Pakistan, which obtains arms from China, France, the United Kingdom and other countries, and that the United States will not supply "massive" amounts of arms or affect the balance. Regrettably he did not explain why the United States would not be better off to continue to embargo, hold aloof from the political confrontation, and focus its efforts on humanitarian and developmental activities. The Carter administration's decision in 1977 to refuse Pakistan's request to buy aircraft is in keeping with U.S. interest in good relations with India and resisting envelopment in any new South Asian imbroglio.[16]

15. "Secretary Kissinger's News Conference of February 23," *Department of State Bulletin*, Mar. 17, 1975, p. 322.

16. Bernard Weinraub, "U.S. Withholds Sale of Jets to Pakistan," *New York Times*, June 3, 1977.

Allies in Latin America

After World War II the United States supplied most Latin American arms, mainly by grants of equipment from surplus stocks.[17] The essential concern was hemispheric defense. In the early 1960s, emphasis shifted to counterinsurgency, in response to Cuban support of insurgent activities. Latin American military authorities, as the 1960s progressed, increasingly insisted on purchasing new equipment to replace obsolete and often inoperable World War II aircraft, ships, and other weaponry. Their interest in modern arms purchases met powerful opposition in the United States.

Such purchases were criticized as wasteful and unnecessary, in view of the decline of a visible external military threat and the inappropriateness of major equipment for counterinsurgency programs. Some supporters of Latin American economic development questioned the use of U.S. economic aid for such nonproductive purposes and even argued against U.S. contributions to international lending organs because military purchases meant a diversion of local resources and external aid. As a result, government credit for sales of sophisticated equipment was banned, a ceiling was put on the total amount of aid and sales, and economic aid was to be curtailed when local resources or external aid were "unnecessarily" diverted to "excessive" military expenditures.

In Latin America these restrictions were viewed as officious and paternalistic, and purchasers turned to Britain, France, and West Germany, which before World War II had been major sources of arms, and to Canada. Orders estimated to have totaled $1.3 billion, or 83.5 percent of Latin American military purchases (excluding Cuba), went to Europe and Canada in fiscal 1968–72.[18] Clearly, U.S. legislative restrictions did not lower the level of arms acquisitions but simply redirected them to other suppliers, as the executive branch and industry spokesmen lost no opportunity to point out. Congress in the 1970s first raised the ceiling on arms transfers to Latin America, then exempted cash sales, and in 1974 abolished the ceiling entirely.

17. For the evolving pattern of U.S. military aid to Latin America, see AID, *U.S. Loans and Grants and Assistance from International Organizations: Obligations and Authorizations, July 1, 1945–June 30, 1976* (AID, 1977), p. 33.

18. Luigi Einaudi and others, *Arms Transfers to Latin America: Toward a Policy of Mutual Respect,* R-1173-DOS (Santa Monica, Calif.: Rand Corp., 1973), p. 13.

The United States ought now to allow sales of conventional military equipment and services to Latin American countries on a nondiscriminatory, cash basis, consistent with U.S. political and security criteria. Military aid is not justified since there is no clear external threat to Latin America, insurgent movements have shrunk to manageable proportions, and Cuba has adopted a more conciliatory posture toward its neighbors. Particular legislative restrictions should not be imposed on sales; they should not be actively promoted or encouraged, however.

There is little reason to believe that the removal of restrictive guidelines would spur an arms race. Military expenditures in Latin America are lower as a share of national resources than in any other region of the world except Africa, and are not rising. While rivalries between Brazil and Argentina, between Chile and Peru, and between Colombia and Venezuela introduce a competitive element into arms purchases, other demands on resources compete with claims for arms. Latin American arms imports rose from $126 million in 1966 to $437 million in 1975, but much of this was due to inflation. Arms imports amounted to 6.4 percent of military expenditures in 1966 and 6.9 percent in 1975, but less than 0.2 percent of gross national product both years.[19] The United States, of course, should continue to accord priority to development. In any case, it is not likely to recover its dominant position as arms supplier to Latin America. The general trend of Latin American trade is toward diversification of trading partners, and recent experience in the arms field, plus a pervasive concern about U.S. hegemony, will cause reluctance to become again dependent on a single supplier. In a more mature and equal relationship between the United States and Latin America, a role for Western European countries as arms suppliers and advisers should not contravene any important U.S. interest.

To avoid promoting arms sales, credit should be made available only for security-related sales. Internal budgetary pressures and competition for resources should be allowed to act as a discipline on Latin American arms appetites, without easy credit to weight internal decisions. If arms purchases on favorable credit terms from Britain or France should become the prevailing pattern, that is preferable to U.S. use of government credit to promote arms sales, which could lead again into the tangle of arbitrary ceilings and politically controversial allocations.

19. Calculated from data in Arms Control and Disarmament Agency (ACDA), *World Military Expenditures and Arms Transfers, 1966–1975* (GPO, 1976).

Such a policy eases the difficulty of managing U.S. relations with Latin American military regimes, whose interest and competence in guiding modernization, and whose repressiveness, vary widely. The legislative proscription is clear-cut against sales by the United States that would have the effect of arming dictators who are denying fundamental rights or social progress to their own people. The dilemma of dealing with authoritarian regimes will be obviated by a balanced, nonpromotional, nonhortatory approach that excludes the use of arms sales as a major instrument of foreign policy in Latin America. The United States would thus be free to develop constructive relations with military leaders, dealing with them as with any duly constituted government, taking into account how their policies affect U.S. interests, their relations with their neighbors, and any special matters such as their practices related to human rights.

While the United States should avoid a patronizing approach that would suggest what arms Latin American countries need and can afford, U.S. political interests should dictate what sales would be unacceptable for the United States. If the sale of arms to one state would clearly appear threatening to a neighbor, and might strain U.S. relations with that neighbor or force the United States to sell corresponding weapons to it, the United States should stand aside. Similarly, it should withhold weapons used primarily for crowd control or clearly intended for the forcible maintenance in power of a repressive regime. The clear intent of U.S. policy should be to avoid or contain and settle disputes and conflicts; and states of the region should be aware that in pursuit of that objective, the United States will suspend deliveries of weapons and other military equipment.

As a corollary to that intention, the United States should phase out security assistance to Latin America. Grant aid could be terminated promptly, since there is no imminent external threat and only minor insurgencies that might justify aid. Moreover, it is a dubious instrument of political influence and bargaining in the current uneasy U.S.-Latin American relationships. The United States might also phase out government credits for arms sales, thus ending all financial inducements to arms purchases. The curtailment of such assistance to Argentina and Uruguay in early 1977 out of human rights considerations was a move in this direction. Retaliation against infringement of human rights in countries such as Argentina and Brazil with flourishing domestic arms industries may simply encourage them to expand.

Middle East Combatants

Israel, Egypt, Syria, and Jordan have been combatants in as many as four wars since the establishment of Israel as a state. None is a formal ally of the United States, but all four, and at times Lebanon, have been given security assistance in furtherance of the major U.S. effort to preserve the peace, buttress the security of Israel, maintain good relations with Arab states, and achieve a fair and enduring settlement of Arab–Israeli differences.

Ultimately the Middle East problem must be solved through a negotiated settlement; until then, both sides must be restrained from attempting to impose a solution through conclusive military victory. The Arabs especially must be held in check since Israel could not survive a military defeat (whereas the Arabs have weathered a succession of defeats over three decades). A militarily strong Israel will be requisite for a number of years after a final peace settlement is achieved, as well as during the life of any interim agreement.

The United States must continue to supply Israel with arms at least as sophisticated as the Arabs'. In periods of active hostility, ammunition and other expendable items, spare parts, and replacement equipment must be promptly available. On the other hand, the United States should not encourage American firms to enter into coproduction agreements with Israel. In the past, helping Israel to meet its military requirements has meant large annual appropriations for aid and for credits for arms purchases, as well as forgiveness of $1.5 billion in emergency credits extended during the 1973 war.[20] Continuation of such generous support for Israel provides the military means for assuring that the Arabs do not have a reasonable hope of a military alternative to peace and to a just and lasting settlement; it provides at the same time a political symbol of timely and unwavering U.S. support, with varying meaning for Israelis, Arabs, and the Soviet Union.

Almost as well understood and accepted is the U.S. posture toward the Arabs: an intention to avoid polarization among the Arabs and to keep open and improve prospects for serious negotiation, accommodation, and settlement of the Arab-Israeli conflict. The United States has long-standing commercial and other ties with many Arab states and peoples,

20. Emergency Security Assistance Act of 1973, 87 Stat. 836.

an immediate interest in maintaining the flow of oil (to its allies and the developing nations as well as itself), and a sympathy with Arab antipathy to communism and Soviet influence. Evenhandedness thus matches both U.S. sentiment and U.S. interests. Not until 1976 did this evenhandedness extend to a readiness to sell military equipment to Egypt. For a number of years, however, the United States has sought through aid and sales to influence Jordan.

Such assistance is generally understood to be an effective instrument of foreign and security policy; nevertheless, it involves delicate and difficult decisions. The amount of aid and arms to Arab states must be gauged to preserve evenhandedness and serve its immediate purpose without tipping the balance against Israel and actually providing arms to attack or defeat her. Arms supplied to Israel must be unquestionably adequate, but not great enough to be viewed as a substitute for negotiation toward a final settlement—or to drive the Arabs having good relations with the USSR to escalate their weapons store and the destructiveness of their warfare. Decisions in this delicate matter must be taken in a balanced way, despite their complexity, the attendant disputes in the United States, and the strains on relations between supplier and recipient.

Time and changing balances of power are also a factor in the equation. The effectiveness of Arab fighting forces reached a markedly improved level in 1973. There is no reason to think that the gap in efficiency between them and Israel will not be continually narrowed; the difference rather will lie increasingly in their arms inventories. Arab coordination has also improved, both among front-line countries and with their more distant backers. Oil money is also available. The cost for Israel of future military victories will increase and the assurance of ability to protect Israeli cities and territory will decline. If the time comes when U.S. arms do not suffice to enable Israel to protect itself, the United States will no longer be able to defer the agonizing decision of how large its protective role should be.

Difficult decisions abound in the case of Jordan, whose survival has depended largely on external support from the United Kingdom, the United States, and other Arab nations. To insure his continued rule, King Hussein has on occasion been obliged to adjust his relations with domestic groups and foreign powers—contributing, as a result, to uncertainty regarding future Jordanian policies and state behavior.

Jordanian political life has revolved around problems of integrating

Palestinian Arabs, most of whom are refugees, into a society dominated by East Bank Jordanians who rely on support from Bedouin tribes. In the absence of domestic turmoil or crises with Israel, Jordan was able to attract the loyalty of some Palestinians and the political quiescence of most others. However, after the 1967 Arab defeat, the loss of the West Bank to Israel, and the emergence of the Palestinian commando movement as a major political force in the West Bank and the Arab world generally, King Hussein went on the defensive. He was compelled to crush the Fatah organization in Jordan in 1970–71 because it threatened his rule, but at the cost of a major confrontation with neighboring Syria and the temporary loss of financial support from the Arab oil-producing states.

Recognizing that King Hussein represented a voice of moderation in Arab councils, and wishing to support his efforts to secure control over the activities of the Palestinian commando movement at home, the U.S. government agreed to finance a three-year program to modernize the Jordanian military. In 1971 the United States began to sell sophisticated weapons and fighter aircraft to Jordan.[21] At the same time, the king expanded the army, further multiplying defense costs. And his military representatives soon requested an additional $1.4 billion in military assistance to purchase advanced detection equipment, missiles, and aircraft, which could be used against Israel as well as Syria. The significant boost in Jordan's combat capabilities raises questions about the logic and consistency of U.S. policy. For example, the United States plans to construct a tank rebuilding facility for Jordan. In the case of an ally that the United States helps arm and protect against a common rival or threat this might be an "efficient" project. In the case of Jordan, however, the "threat" includes Israel.

What future role is King Hussein expected to play in the Middle East political arena? Should the United States transform a modest force into a potent military establishment? What are the foreign policy implications of doing so, given Israeli sensitivities and vulnerabilities? Should the United States continue to meet the budgetary shortfalls that would result? Can the financial and military burden be shared with the United Kingdom, or with moderate Arab states that are able to help? Should the United States seek to remain the primary supplier of arms to Jordan even as Jordan becomes an increasingly capable participant in future hostilities? Such questions can only be answered in the context of U.S. Middle

21. *New York Times*, Apr. 8, 1971, and Apr. 1, 1972.

Eastern policy. The prospects for a permanent or partial settlement of the Arab-Israeli conflict, the responsibilities the United States undertakes, and the possible benefits and risks of arms sales must be viewed in this broad framework.

The question of U.S. arms sales to Egypt raises even sharper dilemmas. The break in Egypt's military and arms supply relationships with Russia in late 1975 and early 1976 introduced new fluidity into Middle East political processes. The moderate and realistic Anwar Sadat offered a prospect of greater flexibility in pursuit of a settlement. For Sadat, however, new sources of arms supply were imperative to maintain the military balance with Israel and with rival Arab states such as Libya and Syria, and to protect himself at home from charges that he had put his country in an unarmed and ineffective position. Money was a secondary problem; Saudi Arabia and other wealthy Arab states would assist. Finding suitable suppliers was the crux. Even finding spare parts for Soviet equipment was difficult as the Soviet Union vetoed sales by such licensees as India; some small help was eventually forthcoming from China, however.

The most attractive and reliable supplier in Sadat's eyes was the United States, though he made urgent overtures also to the French, British, Germans, and others. Keeping Egypt free of Soviet ties, and keeping the moderate Sadat in power and disposed to pursue negotiation and accommodation were the purpose of the principle of evenhandedness between Arabs and Israel. The first sale of equipment brought outcries from Israel and its supporters in the United States, but probably no greater than were foreseen.

Practical considerations going to the very heart of the Middle East negotiating process, and the U.S.-Egyptian relationship, pose serious doubts as to the wisdom of more than minor U.S. sales to Egypt. There are risks in the United States' taking on the role of arms supplier. So long as Sadat remains in power, and negotiations and mutual accommodation move ahead, objections to U.S. arms deliveries can probably be shunted aside. The Middle East is a hard and uncertain place, however. Sadat may be replaced by a less compromising or an uncertain figure; crises in Arab-Israeli relations may erupt; even resumption of hostilities is a possibility. Can the United States continue regular supplies of arms under such circumstances? If hostilities break out, how will the principle of evenhandedness work out? The United States will surely keep Israeli stocks up, but can it simultaneously airlift parts and ammunition to

Egypt, or move to rebuild Egyptian inventories promptly after a cease-fire? Failure to do so will put the same kinds of strains on the U.S.-Egyptian relationship, and on Sadat, that ended the Soviet-Egyptian rapport. The U.S.-Egyptian rapprochement, which emerged despite past U.S. arms transfers to Israel, can hardly survive a continuation of the special supply relationship with Israel at a time when supplies to Egypt are cut off. Hard-headed recognition and appraisal of the risks of such an outcome should precede any further consideration of assuming the role of principal arms supplier to Egypt.

A serious search should be made for alternatives. The obvious one is a return to France and Britain as Egypt's principal arms suppliers. The British and French appear to be willing and able to assume the role, and neither has as special a relationship to Israel or as delicate a position in the negotiating process as the United States has. Allowing U.S. corporations to join with British firms in refurbishing—but not in improving on—Egypt's Soviet-supplied aircraft seems incongruous considering the U.S. supply of arms to Israel, but this action is not insensible. The United States could continue the economic, political, and technical cooperation and the security supporting assistance by which it has knit the relationship with Egypt.

Persian Gulf States

Unlike the combatants in the Arab–Israeli conflict, the Arab oil-producing countries and Iran are not dependent on military aid. Moreover, there is no well-articulated U.S. arms policy toward the states in the Persian Gulf. The United States has several quite specific interests in this region—in the continued flow of oil at stable prices; in the limitation of Soviet influence and exclusion of Soviet preeminence; and in avoiding involvement in disputes in the area, which could lead to confrontation with the Soviet Union.

There has been a massive flow of U.S. arms to this region since 1973, and the obscurity of the policy behind it has raised misgivings. Some critics are repelled by the U.S. role of arms purveyor; others wonder whether arms sales contribute to stability or instead feed rivalries and instability, and carry a risk of U.S. involvement in proportion to the U.S. role as arms supplier. Becoming a major supplier, particularly of equipment requiring a substantial U.S. presence for training and maintenance, moves the relationship closer to one of mutual dependence and increases the likelihood of U.S. involvement in any crisis involving a client.

In the absence of a clear declaration of U.S. interests and policies in the Gulf, and of how arms sales fit in, misgivings will persist that the United States is motivated by short-term economic benefits and an over-valuation of what arms can do for regional stability and U.S. influence. Such misgivings were not reduced by hints from Secretary of State Kissinger and Secretary of Defense Schlesinger in the Ford administration regarding the possibility of strong U.S. action, not excluding use of force, to keep oil flowing in event of crisis—while the United States offered its most modern weapons to the very states at which that force would have been directed. The Carter administration has not acted very differently, being willing to conclude major arms sales agreements with Iran and Saudi Arabia.[22]

France and Britain also supply arms to the Middle East and have a large backlog of orders from the Gulf states, and the Soviet Union continues to supply Iraq. Traditional states, where the authority and prestige of rulers are based on force, have a sudden accumulation of wealth that gives them both something concrete to protect and the money to buy arms. Past deliveries of advanced aircraft from the United States and the Soviet Union to Iran and Iraq have established a level from which to proceed to more modern and sophisticated aircraft, missiles, tanks, electronic gear, helicopters, and ships. While the process is more diffuse than the U.S.-Soviet contest to outdo each other's strategic forces, it is none the less an arms race: the defense requirements of the states involved are loosely rather than rigorously and analytically defined, and thus the specific impulses to acquisition are emulation of neighbors and rivals, and perceived need for corresponding counters to a neighbor's strike capability—as Kuwait has sought interceptors, or Iraq and Iran have reciprocally moved to more advanced strike aircraft, interceptors, and antiaircraft weapons. In Saudi Arabia and Iran a quite separate impulse to arm is the need to insure the support of armed forces for rulers in power. Concern about rebellious tribes (such as the Kurds in Iraq) and the

22. DSAA, "Security Assistance Program, Volume 1, FY 1978," p. 19. Foreign military sales orders from the area in fiscal 1977 were estimated at $7.6 billion. DSAA, "Foreign Military Sales and Military Assistance Facts, December 1977" (DSAA, 1978; processed), p. 1. See also *New York Times*, July 12, 1977, and Feb. 15, 1978.

maintenance of order and authority as traditional societies face the complexities of the modern world are also motivating forces.

The drive for arms is strongly sustained; the resistance to it is weak. The Western suppliers (the United States, the United Kingdom, and France), under the strain of either a deficit in their international accounts or sharply risen expenditures for oil imports, have been interested in access to a broader market for goods and services in the oil-producing countries, and arms sales are an entering wedge. Current circumstances reinforce past tendencies among suppliers to compete rather than to act with restraint to avoid arms buildups in sensitive areas. The Soviet Union supplies a great variety of military equipment for political ends to Iraq, and a narrow selection to Iran. A damping down of the arms buildup can be expected only as the appetites and digestive capacities of the buyers are satisfied, not from cooperative restraint by sellers. The limited oil resources of the sheikdoms and the enormous development requirements of Iraq and Iran are likely to slow down purchases; in fact, such a slowdown is already apparent in Iran. Only Saudi Arabia appears to have no limit on what it can afford to acquire.

The upward spiral in the number and sophistication of arms is not the cause of the tensions and rivalries in the region, nor will arms acquisitions necessarily increase the likelihood that a conflict will erupt. Instability and rivalry are endemic in the region. There have been confrontations or clashes between Iraq and Kuwait, and between Iraq and Iran, as well as general Arab uneasiness about Iranian ambitions toward hegemony in the area and control over the Gulf and the Strait of Hormuz. Yemen has supported a rebellion in Oman, while Saudi Arabia and Iran have supported the sultan. There are latent instabilities (for example, the currently suppressed Kurdish insurgency in Iraq and the succession in Iran); and there remains the general problem of movement from traditional to modern societies and governments in Saudi Arabia and the sheikhdoms. There are ties with external conflicts—the Moslem sympathies of Arabs and Iran for Pakistan in its rivalry with India, and Saudi Arabia's and Iraq's involvement in the Arab-Israeli conflict. The United States has as clients Iran and Saudi Arabia, and the USSR has Iraq, as well as ties in Yemen and elsewhere on the peninsula; the British and French have historic ties and current commercial interests in the area. Most pervasive of all is the confrontation of the oil producers with the established industrial world over the price of petroleum and broader issues of relations between industrialized and developing states.

These rivalries and instabilities antedate the current arms buildup. It is doubtful that arms will help in stabilizing matters. In a crisis, it is conceivable that one party might resort to arms either to exploit a perceived superiority or to deny its rival time to build up its forces for such an attack later. Fortunately, the trend has been toward improved relations and the settlement of disputes (as between Iraq and Kuwait, Iraq and Iran, and Iran and the sheikhdoms). Arms transfers and development of military balances have had little effect on this trend. More influential have been the pressure of internal development and social problems and the need to apply resources to them; a preference, since the British withdrawal, for settling differences without calling on major powers or offering an occasion for intervention; and a habit of working together—sometimes with considerable success—in OPEC and Arab councils and of being urged by these organs to resolve their differences. The trend is an encouraging one, though old disputes and rivalries are unlikely to disappear quickly and permanently. The direction is right, however—toward a regional subsystem developed by accommodation among the states of the area.

Nevertheless, there is no escaping the difficult questions of how many and what kinds of arms should be sold to the Gulf states, particularly Iran and Saudi Arabia. In 1977 Iran's request to order a modified version of a U.S. fighter aircraft was rejected on the ground that it would encourage the development of arms for export. The administration also refused a large order for a type of aircraft the Iranians had previously purchased. But it supported Iran's purchase of an advanced airborne-warning-and-control-system aircraft and its support systems. Though the latter aircraft is not a weapon system itself, it can markedly increase the efficiency of combat aircraft; moreover, it incorporates the most advanced avionics in the world. The possibility that the USSR might try by reward or covert operation to obtain this new technology raises questions about Iranian security. The major task for the United States now is to persuade Iran that it has enough weaponry to insure its security against all neighboring states except the USSR, and that a marginally greater stock of arms is of less value in its relations with the Soviet Union than are U.S. friendship and support and in the long run could lead to regional instability.

One problem in U.S. sales of military equipment to Iran that has concerned many members of Congress is Iran's dependence on U.S. military and civilian personnel for the operation and maintenance of the equipment. "The number of official and private American citizens in Iran, a large percentage of whom are involved in military programs, has . . . increased from approximately 15,000–16,000 in 1972 to 24,000 in 1976; it could easily reach 50,000–60,000 or higher by 1980."[23] If Iran found its way into a conflict, the work done by U.S. personnel might be essential to the Iranian military effort. Denial of this support could mean disaster for Iran and certainly would strain U.S. relations. But allowing these personnel to support Iran could involve the United States even though its interests were better served by remaining on the sidelines.

The same issue presents itself in sales to Saudi Arabia and only compounds the difficulty of making decisions about sales to a country that might use arms against Israel. Past agreements with Saudi Arabia have been heavily related to the construction of military infrastructure. In the years to come, though, Saudi Arabia will want to purchase increasingly advanced aircraft, ground vehicles, and perhaps warships. Already the executive has announced its willingness to sell the U.S. Air Force's most advanced fighter aircraft, the F-15, to Saudi Arabia, which clearly is not capable of operating and maintaining it. Since Saudi Arabia seems unwilling to accept restrictions against use of U.S.-supplied weapons against Israel, the United States should decline unrestricted sales, notwithstanding U.S. economic interests and the probability that Britain and France will otherwise seek to fill this void. On the other hand, if an Arab–Israeli peace settlement should be achieved and be strongly supported by Saudi Arabia, moderate sales would not be out of order.

African Nations

The major suppliers of arms to Africa have been the Soviet Union and France; the U.S. share in the period 1966–75 was only 11 percent.[24] The security assistance programs that have existed in recent years have been small, totaling only $58 million in fiscal 1976.[25] Sales have also been low, with the exception of orders totaling nearly $300 million by Morocco in

23. *U.S. Military Sales to Iran*, staff report to the Senate Committee on Foreign Relations, 94:2 (GPO, 1976), p. vii.
24. ACDA, *World Military Expenditures and Arms Transfers, 1966–1975*, p. 79.
25. DSAA, "Security Assistance Program, Volume 1, FY 1978," pp. 25 and 235.

fiscal 1975.[26] Even Zaire, where the United States was heavily involved in the early 1960s and has remained a supplier of arms, received only nonlethal materiel while suffering invasion by insurgents from Angola in 1977. The U.S. security assistance program for Ethiopia, which dragged on until 1977, is an almost classic example of inability to end a program and a dramatic illustration of some of the dilemmas of the arms supply relationship.

United States military assistance to Ethiopia was closely tied to the permission accorded to the United States to operate the Kagnew communications station, located at Asmara in the northernmost province of Ethiopia. The status of the installation, which had been set up in World War II, was regularized on May 22, 1953,[27] when a mutual defense assistance agreement was signed. An accompanying military assistance agreement represented payment for U.S. basing and operating rights in Ethiopia.

In the 1960s, operations at Kagnew began to be phased down as dissident movements in Ethiopia grew. But ties with Emperor Haile Selassie's government became increasingly strong. Ethiopia's role as a moderating influence in the Organization of African Unity and its strategic position adjacent to the Red Sea–Persian Gulf–Indian Ocean area were deemed sufficient reason for continuing a relatively high level of military assistance. The United States became virtually Ethiopia's sole supplier and trained and helped to organize its armed forces.

After the Selassie government was toppled in September 1974, U.S. policymakers continued to regard Ethiopia as a client state to which the United States had an obligation. The level of military aid and sales credits rose appreciably following the military coup. The rationale for continuing aid was that to terminate all assistance would alienate the emerging leadership and might be regarded by other nations dependent on the United States as their primary source of military supply as an indication of irresolution in a friend or ally. Moreover, failure of authority at Addis Ababa, it was feared, might encourage insurrection by ethnic and tribal minorities in other areas of East Africa. Yet the United States had virtually no capacity to influence the new military council to follow a

26. DSAA, *Foreign Military Sales and Military Assistance Facts, December 1976* (DSAA, 1977), p. 13.

27. 4 UST (United States Treaties and Other International Agreements) 421; Treaties and International Acts Series 2787.

moderate political course in dealing with the Eritrean separatists. Further conspicuous infusions of U.S. arms and ammunition ran the risk of antagonizing the Eritreans and the Arab governments that supplied them with financial support and materiel. The alternatives and options before the U.S. government were narrow and unattractive. On the other hand, the advantages of continued security assistance and liberal arms supplies were difficult to perceive. No changes were made, however, until 1977, when President Carter curtailed assistance because of concern about human rights.[28] In response to this action the Ethiopian government unilaterally terminated the 1953 mutual defense agreement and ordered the U.S. military assistance advisory group and the personnel operating the Kagnew station to leave the country.[29]

The Ethiopian experience should be clear warning that in future decisions regarding arms supply the United States should be careful not to fall into a position of allowing other countries or regimes—particularly unstable ones in areas of tension—to become dependent on the United States. The de facto responsibility for another country's ability to defend itself forces the United States to support causes or governments in which it has no interest.

The question of military assistance to Somalia is a case in point. After the United States withdrew from Ethiopia, the Soviet Union and Cuba began to provide for Ethiopia's security needs. At the same time the USSR began to hold back on arms transfers to Somalia which was pressing its territorial claims through military actions in the Ogaden region in Ethiopia. Eventually Somalia expelled Soviet and Cuban personnel and terminated the Soviet Union's use of valuable military facilities. When Somalia began to look around in 1977 for other sources of arms, the United States at first seemed favorably disposed to offer security assistance as a counter to Soviet influence in Ethiopia. But that would have meant lending support to the idea of territorial change by force in a continent, indeed a world, laden with claims for border adjustments. A wiser strategy, serving long-term U.S. interests, would be to encourage Somalian trade and cultural relationships with the West. If Somalia works out its differences with Ethiopia in an acceptable way—for example, through

28. Bernard Gwertzman, "U.S. Cuts Foreign Aid in Rights Violations; South Korea Exempt," *New York Times*, Feb. 25, 1977.
29. *Washington Post*, Apr. 24, 1977.

mediation by the Organization of African Unity—the United States might then consider arms transfers satisfying the country's legitimate defense needs. An even wiser course would be to look favorably upon moderate European sales.

As another result of the developing Soviet–Cuban presence in Ethiopia, the United States in late 1977 indicated its willingness to sell a small number of combat aircraft to Sudan. It was not apparent that the country faced any military threat. The administration seemed concerned to show U.S. interest in the Horn area of Africa and to give some symbolic support to Sudan. Similar factors had led to the sale of planes to Kenya a year earlier. Unlike Kenya, though, Sudan could conceivably offer these aircraft for use against Israel in a new conflict.

The small size of these sales and the types of aircraft involved are reasonable in terms of the motivating factors. In the Sudan case particularly, though, the United States must be careful not to whet an appetite for purchases and should obtain agreement, insured by practical efforts, that the aircraft will not be used for any purpose other than defense. The delivery of these weapons should be contingent on the continuation of the current political constellations in Egypt and Sudan.

An International Approach to Arms Decisions

The United States does not, of course, define its concern with the security of other countries only according to its direct interests in a particular locale. As a founding member of the United Nations, the United States has accepted the obligation of all members "to maintain international peace and security, and to that end: to take effective collective measures for the prevention and removal of threats to the peace, and for the suppression of acts of aggression or other breaches of the peace."[30] Moreover, as a permanent member of the Security Council, it is charged with "primary responsibility for the maintenance of international peace and security."[31]

During early years of the United Nations when the divisiveness of the cold war and the emergence of a Third World majority made it difficult

30. *Charter of the United Nations* (GPO, 1945), art. 1, p. 3.
31. Ibid., art. 24, p. 10.

to maintain peace and security, the United States sought to fulfill its responsibilities with regard to international peace and the suppression of aggression—both seen as vital to its own security—by recourse to regional arrangements and the "inherent right of individual or collective self-defense" as recognized in the UN Charter.[32]

The United States continues to have a major role in maintaining international security and peace, but power is now more diffuse, the overall balance is more intricate and stable, and conflicts are predominantly local or regional. The economic power of Japan, the European Community, and OPEC has increasing weight and relevance in international affairs. Thus, except where its major allies and Israel are concerned, the United States can approach local threats to the peace as one member of the international community, as it did in the Nigerian civil war, for example. When U.S. allies are embroiled with each other (as Greece and Turkey, Honduras and El Salvador have been), the United States can best approach the conflict as a member—even if the most powerful one—of NATO, the Organization of American States, or the UN Security Council. It thereby involves other nations that properly share responsibility and puts the weight of a consensus of allies and neighbors behind restoring peace and effecting conciliation.

One of the statutory purposes of U.S. security assistance or arms sales is to support UN peace efforts and the contribution that other states make to those efforts. When incipient or actual conflict could involve the superpowers, mediation or other resolution of disputes through the United Nations and through consultation between the major powers might keep the conflict in bounds and reduce the chances of political or military confrontation between the superpowers. At a minimum, it would identify U.S. purposes with those of the UN Charter and fix international concerns as the cause of any subsequent unilateral measures (arms or political or other support) the United States might find it necessary to use to aid a threatened party.

A broader consideration that has affected U.S. foreign policy planning in the last few years is the gap in income between the "haves" and "have-nots" in the world. When the United States has a choice, priority in future aid programs should go to development assistance over security assistance. Security when threatened, however, is an overriding pre-

32. Ibid., arts. 51 and 52, pp. 17–18.

occupation; U.S. efforts therefore should focus on creating an international political environment in which tension and hostility are reduced so that a minimum amount of local resources or external aid will be needed for military purposes. Conflicts and perceptions of threats often lead nations to allocate resources to military expenditures and arms purchases, as the Arab–Israeli rivals, the countries of Southeast Asia, Pakistan, and Ethiopia have done. Military expenditures by, and U.S. arms sales to other poor countries—even those with military regimes in Africa and Latin America—have been consistently low. The United States should work to reduce tension and settle disputes through diplomatic efforts rather than encouraging military self-reliance; such a course would be cheaper for these nations in the short run and more stabilizing in the long run.

In the years ahead, U.S. security interests will sometimes be mutually reinforcing and sometimes conflicting. Protecting direct American interests and those shared with allies will continue to be a prime concern. But maintaining international peace and security generally and creating conditions favorable to self-determination should be a constant goal. And avoiding involvement in conflict—for the sake of protecting American lives and economic security, but also in the hope of containing violence and promoting the shared responsibility of other nations—should be an operating premise of U.S. policy. Where other powerful nations are concerned, the United States will want to avoid confrontation, yet neither will it wish to see hegemony established in the Third World. Among nations dependent on U.S. or Soviet arms or protection, it should encourage self-reliance and regional cooperation. And among others it should encourage minimal military expenditures and establishments and discourage preoccupation with military power and arms.

Human rights, economic development and the wider availability of necessities of life, and peaceful pursuits should have priority over arms transfers in U.S. dealings with other nations. The United States should not offer security aid or take military or political action without carefully considering whether the intervention is necessary and what others can do, what the costs of intervening and standing aside will be, and what the alternative, more political approaches are.

A number of countries whose natural resources, rate of growth, and size portend a larger regional or world role in the future will be of particular interest to the United States. Iran, Egypt, Brazil, Venezuela, Mexico, Argentina, Nigeria, and Indonesia either have rich essential resources, such as deposits of petroleum and copper, or are moving toward balanced development and industrialization. In establishing and maintaining a mutually beneficial relationship with these states the United States may want to offer its security resources. But these countries in general will not need security assistance. They will be interested, however, in the role of U.S. military forces in regional stability and the regional balance of power, and they will probably wish to buy U.S. arms and in some cases U.S. technology and equipment to build their own armed forces.

Those emerging nations that do not already have security ties with the United States will probably not seek formal U.S. security guarantees. A diplomacy of independence will better match their aspirations and in most cases will not be a luxury. Nevertheless, these states are likely to see U.S. military power as essential to the security of the world and to the regional environment in which they can pursue their own development with safety. They will want a sufficiently close relationship with the United States to permit them to be confident that their security and related requirements are weighed when U.S. foreign policy and military plans are formulated.

For the United States an informal understanding that is consistent with U.S. security policies may be advantageous for a number of reasons. It represents a mature association between politically equal states and thus circumvents the dependent or client relationship of the militarily weaker state in a security agreement. It permits priority to be given to economic, technical, and social advance. By promoting independence and self-determination, it encourages the rising state to be responsible for determining its own defense requirements and capacity for financing armed forces and arms purchases and puts any arms transfer or production arrangements on a healthy footing. It leaves the United States free to reexamine its interests when power shifts among neighboring states; if weaker states become dominated or threatened militarily or politically by a growing neighbor, new demands for military aid or for political or military support may arise for the United States.

An informal security relationship somewhat insulates the United States, so that it can maintain normal diplomatic relationships and pursue common interests without being closely identified with an unpopular or short-lived regime. And without a formal security alliance, the United

States can seek to involve other states politically in actions calculated to ease regional tensions, build constructive relations, and contribute to broader cooperation in economic, security, or peacekeeping activities.

Requests by other nations to purchase arms will be handled best if they are examined in terms of their individual merits. Blanket policies will almost certainly not be helpful to U.S. interests abroad. On the other hand, a policy that seeks to bridge the gaps between the conflicting interests related to arms transfers will require a high level of statecraft and diplomatic skill as well as a large supply of political savvy at home.

CHAPTER SIX

Selectivity and Moderation

One course of action the United States might elect to take toward the world traffic in arms is to put a strict and low limit on exports of military goods and services and seek to stand aside from the worldwide preoccupation with security and the attendant pursuit of military equipment. Such a choice of policy is unlikely, however, and uncharacteristic of the postwar U.S. view of its role in international affairs. It certainly would not transform the arms trade. The active arms market is kept alive by old and new rivalries and ambitions and disputes among the nations of a splintered world. The great majority of states import arms from one or more of the major supplier countries. For countries with cash to pay, it is likely to remain a buyer's market for some time. Western countries with excess or easily expandable arms production have an active interest in foreign markets in a time of economic strain; in the Soviet Union, arms development and production is probably the most modern and efficient economic sector, and sales of arms have traditionally been used for political purposes.

The U.S. role in supply of arms is in reasonable proportion to the United States' technical and industrial standing in the world and especially its predominance in the production of technologically advanced goods.[1] Nor does the United States foist arms on the needy: only 1 percent of U.S. arms sales over the past twenty-five years have gone to the forty-eight poorest or neediest countries and over four-fifths of that went

1. According to an estimate provided by the Aerospace Industries Association of America on March 29, 1977, 81 percent of all civil aircraft ranging from helicopters and single engine planes to jet transports, are American made; over 90 percent of all jet transports are American made.

to India and Pakistan alone.[2] The rise in U.S. arms transfers—primarily to wealthy Persian Gulf and Middle East states—is a reflection of generally rising military expenditures by developing states that must import their arms.

The United States is not likely to move precipitately out of this trade. Nor is it likely to allow the commercialization of the U.S. traffic in arms by putting sales in private hands. A shift from governmental to commercial channels in the promotion of arms sales would not lead to less aggressiveness; rather the opposite could be expected. Nor would a shift depoliticize arms sales. Indeed, the U.S. government would be open to accusations of manipulating corporate arms exporters as its agents. The U.S. government may give up authority, but it cannot abdicate its responsibility. The grounds for meeting its responsibility and the prospects of success are greater if the government retains an active role in arms sales.

Economic motives and calculations are not absent from present U.S. arms sales; they are only subordinate. A change in principle here would signal a radical reversal in U.S. policies on encouragement of economic development, support of collective security, and the pursuit of international peace and stability.

Between the extremes of conceivable U.S. action lie two more nicely balanced courses: one a vigorous and comprehensive security assistance and arms sales program governed by political and security predispositions, the other a rigorous security assistance screening and a more cautious and moderate arms sales policy. The debate about these choices in arms policy, and the related debate about executive and legislative roles and authorities, is part of the larger debate about U.S. defense and foreign policies and the U.S. role they would support.

Although the Carter administration opted in 1977 for a more cautious course, its behavior often belied what its pronouncements implied. The attitudes that underlie the administration's questioning of continued security assistance and its repugnance toward U.S. leadership in arms sales reflect sensible concerns that are of increasing importance. For a constantly larger proportion of Congress, the press, and voters generally, Hitler and Mussolini, World War II, and the generous impulses of col-

2. U.S. Department of Defense, Defense Security Assistance Agency, *Foreign Military Sales and Military Assistance Facts, December 1976* (DSAA, 1977), pp. 12–13.

lective security and the philosophy of U.S. responsibility for worldwide peace, economic recovery, and growth are matters of history rather than experience. They recall Vietnam with its bitterness and disillusionment, not World War II and Korea. Distaste for dictators and military coups is often more active than concern over disorder or insurgency in distant countries.

Unemployment, energy needs, and inflation are urgent domestic problems. In the outside world, making détente work, common action on food and energy problems, more orderly international commercial and financial arrangements are more challenging and interesting tasks than reinforcing alliances built up after World War II or improving the military capabilities of tens of nations and their ruling regimes. And arms sales, even if they bring in welcome export orders, may be eyed askance as presaging future international violence and problems for the United States.

Whatever the tilt that U.S. foreign policy follows in fact, certain trends in arms transfers are already evident. The United States has phased down its security assistance to many countries and has become more selective; while security grants remain large, the biggest bloc of that aid is not for arms or training but for supporting programs. Sales are increasingly the mode used for transferring arms and training—though they may be supported by government credits or guarantees.

The trend toward sales (the greater part for cash) is desirable not just for the beneficial effects of sales on the U.S. budget, foreign-exchange position, and domestic productivity, but for the demand that sales put on the purchasing countries to subject their defense plans and arms purchases to their own budgetary disciplines. So long as the imperative to acquire arms for security prevails, their availability by import is preferable to a spread of industries devoted to arms production, and for developing countries it is less of an economic burden than setting up small, inefficient, and costly production facilities.

Recent rises in the world arms trade and U.S. arms sales do not reflect barometric changes. Arms purchases are under strong pressure, both politically and in budgetary duels with nonmilitary needs, everywhere except in the Middle East where Arab-Israeli hostilities and sudden oil wealth have led to real rises. Increases in dollar value of arms purchases in Western and Eastern Europe, Asia, Africa, and Latin America are largely due to inflation and higher unit costs of sophisticated replacement equipment. Even in the Persian Gulf, weapons orders outpace the capacity to use them (as in Iran and Saudi Arabia), and economic development plans compete for resources because high oil prices have led to lower exports and revenues (as in Iran).

The size of the arms trade is a melancholy fact; like military budgets and armed forces, it is a nonproductive use of resources in a world of widespread hunger and poverty, and a warning sign of future wars and crises. Yet it is a serious misreading of the international situation, and no service to practical efforts to achieve a greater degree of international peace and justice, to view the current arms trade as an aberration or abnormality, or to search for villians. The international trade in arms— over three-fourths involving the developing world—while great, is still considerably smaller than the arms expenditures of the U.S. Department of Defense each year. (Soviet procurement is currently running at an even greater rate.) American arms and military expenditures may appear fully justified because of the threats and the responsibilities the United States must face. Other countries may seem to have more urgent economic and social business to pursue, and fewer dangers to face that justify priority to military things. But to other countries, their environment is no less unstable or insecure, their claims or disputes or rivalries no less peremptory, the reassurance and reinforcement of national identity and pride from an imposing defense establishment no less valued by leaders and the man in the street than are these matters for Americans.

The impulse to trade in arms, then, by no means comes primarily from the supplier countries. Industrial nations add to the pressure on the rest of the world to equip and modernize their forces principally by example—the performance of new weapons (in recent years in Southeast Asia, South Asia, and the Middle East) demonstrates how they outmode older models. So long as the main powers of the industrial world, among themselves and in their many interrelations with the developing world, pursue the development of military technology, to treat the arms trade as an anomalous phenomenon to be rectified independently of major and recalcitrant international problems and issues is self-deception.

The United States will continue to be a major arms supplier over the next few years, then, and should define how it may play this role wisely and responsibly. Despite some major miscalculations, the U.S. sales and security assistance programs have not been basically misguided in either their essential purpose or their execution. These activities, however, have been accorded more weight and trust than they merit; in order is a small selective program of assistance, a judicious and moderate approach to arms sales, and great caution in exporting arms-producing technology.

A sensible arms policy will incorporate a prudent view of the political and security effects of arms transfers, a disposition to see the short-term advantages as less important and the long-term uncertainties and risks as more consequential, and a skepticism about the wisdom or necessity of regarding arms supply (whether by assistance or sales) as a dominant element in U.S. relationships with most of the states that lie outside the Communist world.

Selectivity in Security Assistance

The controversy surrounding U.S. security assistance programs and budget requests tends to obscure wide areas of agreement and clear-cut trends in assistance. The major segment of the program since the Indochina conflict ended relates to the Middle East, where consensus reigns both as to objectives and funding. The value of grants for other areas is declining, particularly if inflation is taken into account, as is the number of clients.

What remains in dispute, other than individual programs or funding levels, is the utility of security assistance as a tool of U.S. foreign policy, and the discretion that the President and secretary of state should have —outside the normal budgetary process—in offering such aid to meet sudden crises in other countries. The difference in attitudes on these matters underlies both the sharp clash in 1976 over aid to factions in Angola and the more long-drawn-out dispute over whether the program should be phased out.

The International Security Assistance and Arms Export Control Act of 1976 set a schedule for the formal closing of a protean activity that began immediately after World War II with the sharp confrontation between free and Communist worlds, each dependent on one superpower for military supplies as well as backing. In a still uneasy but vastly more complex world, it should be the exception rather than the rule for the United States to assume responsibility for the military capabilities of other countries. Most nations should shape their own defense establishments to match what they can afford.

The grant security assistance program is not being ended primarily because of change in U.S. policy or in the U.S. view of its role in the world. It reflects realities such as the collapse of U.S. clients in Indochina, the economic growth of allies or other associates on the periphery of the Communist states as well as elsewhere, and a more diffuse or even divided Communist world pressing less actively on its neighbors and engendering less acute demands for U.S. help in meeting internal or external danger.

The need for U.S. security assistance will not disappear in the near future, however. It will be used to sustain embattled friends (such as Israel); as an instrument of foreign policy (aid to Egypt or Jordan, for example, as well as Israel in pursuit of a full and lasting Middle East settlement); and as a quid pro quo for concessions to the United States (as with base facilities in Spain or the Philippines). Leaving aside the unpredictable Middle East, the program of grants for military assistance should continue to be small. Only a few recipient countries remain highly vulnerable, and during the transitional period as grants to them are being phased out, they could be offered security supporting assistance and credits for arms purchases.

It is difficult to foresee any new and compelling security assistance requirements, even if the luster of détente is somewhat dimmed. Increasingly U.S. allies need and ask not for assistance but for assurance that the massive economic and political as well as military power of the United States will remain committed to common security interests. In the Third World there will continue to be conflicts arising out of rivalries and new or old disputes or clashes of interest; disparities in the wealth and industrialization and power of neighboring states will also be a source of tension. The U.S. policy ought to be to avoid new bilateral military commitments and the dependence they bring; it should instead stress self-determination, leaving with other countries and governments the responsibility for shaping their development programs, their relations with their neighbors, and the size and character of their defense establishments. The U.S. interest in international peace and security can be channeled into the regional or UN security framework—not as a way of avoiding responsibility or of inflating international organs, but to add U.S. power and influence to a larger effort to minimize dominance or confrontation among the great powers in local disputes, and to diffuse and thus make more stable the responsibility for settling disputes and maintaining peace.

The problems of security assistance, of course, are quite unlike those of arms sales. Whether the United States takes an active or a passive stance toward arms sales, its arms customers will include countries with no claim for security aid. Announcement of the impending end of the assistance program will have the salutary effect of turning recipients' planning away from indefinite dependence toward self-reliance. Increasingly, the political aspect of assistance has been the key to U.S. involvement—a symbol of interest and commitment, a gesture of support to the recipient and of warning to its neighbors or to other powerful nations.

Though security assistance may be a useful foreign policy tool, it does not necessarily buy the commodity sought. Neither arms nor other forms of assistance can assure the security of the client. In most cases the amount of aid involved is too small to make more than a marginal military difference. Clearly, however, in the cases of Israel and of Jordan, the security bought has been crucial. But in Indochina the effort to achieve through security assistance a stalemate or victory that could not be achieved by the use of substantial U.S. ground, air, and naval forces seemed to many foredoomed to failure.

In cases such as Turkey and South Korea, the value of security assistance must be judged against an active U.S. defense commitment contained in a treaty, as well as the presence of U.S. forces on the territory or in the area. South Korea is now the only country where substantial U.S. forces are deployed; security assistance there is a reasonable trade-off for the withdrawal of U.S. ground forces. Nevertheless, it cannot be counted on to play as stabilizing a role as visible troop deployments.

In exchange for base rights and facilities, security assistance may represent legitimate and acceptable compensation. In fact, facilities in the Philippines, Turkey, Greece, Spain, and Portugal are compensated in whole or part in this way. Other factors may also carry weight, however, in obtaining the assent of the host country to a U.S. base or a right to use facilities. Thus bases obtained for normal peacetime use may not be available in times of tension—as was the case with bases even on the territory of U.S. NATO allies at the time of the 1973 Arab–Israeli hostility. And bases can become lightning rods even in friendly countries; thus, changing local political tides may lead even formal treaty partners to ask that the United States withdraw some or all of its forces in the country, as happened in Thailand and Greece. Multiyear agreements with Spain, Turkey, Greece, and the Philippines to provide aid in return for bases will probably constitute a major part of future security assistance programs outside the Middle East.

In terms of foreign policy, these agreements raise the question of the wisdom of placing a heavy weight on base facilities and air rights, predominantly military, in working out difficult relations with countries of great importance to the United States. In the case of the Philippines, the political problems involve the U.S. posture toward the authoritarian regime and its actions with regard to human rights, as well as toward Muslim insurgency. If either aspect of the Philippines scene should take an adverse turn, the strong human rights provisions of the 1976 legislation could force a review of the supply of U.S. arms, with repercussions on U.S. base rights. In the case of Spain, the treaty covering bases is broad in scope, including economic as well as military aid.

The most dubious agreements politically are those with Greece and Turkey. The basic problem is to resolve Greek and Turkish differences over Cyprus and other matters, and in doing so to avoid further confrontation and even conflict and to reestablish good relations between the two countries, as well as with the United States and the rest of NATO. Both the bases and the military aid given in exchange may be important, but less so than political stabilization—and they are unlikely to survive if the Greek–Turkish dispute and the attendant friction with the United States continue. The agreements may be intended as part of a step-by-step approach to a political settlement. They are dubious paths, however.

There is bickering about the comparative merits of the two agreements, as each state sees the threat posed by the arms received by its rival as greater than the value of those it receives. And if military moves are renewed, they are highly likely to involve the use, or danger of use, of U.S. arms, with a consequent cutoff or threat of cutoff of deliveries under the supply agreements. Not only good U.S. relations with Greece and Turkey (and prospects for political progress) would be imperiled: again the obvious countermove would be suspension of base rights.

This dilemma points to another anomaly of such accords: they place the value of the facilities not on the mutually maintained common defense, but on an asset for which the United States pays its indifferent allies. This kind of relationship does not bode well for the future health of the Western alliance in the politically sensitive eastern Mediterranean. Nor does bilateral bargaining over military aid related to the multilateral requirements and contributions of NATO powers. In a major Greek–Turkish confrontation that involved U.S.-supplied arms, the damage to U.S. relations with NATO allies would inevitably be great; the best prospect for insulating U.S. bases and minimizing the dangers of political exposure will be to keep NATO ties and interests in the foreground and seek settlement under NATO in preference to U.S. aegis, and in the

United States to develop a posture and strategy that commands effective acceptance and support in Congress and among the interested public.

Security assistance can perhaps play an important part in the overall negotiating approach toward resolution of the stubborn dispute. It cannot play the key role, however, and risks being the occasion for further domestic and international acrimony. And at a time when Greece and Turkey are primarily concerned with their military posture vis-à-vis each other, it can hardly be argued that the Soviet threat to them makes too risky any constraint on the restoration of military aid by the United States.

Though security assistance can on occasion be used as an instrument of political influence or goodwill, arms thus supplied can well outlive the regime they seek to bolster. Political influence bought by such payments in unstable and changing countries is of dubious value, as Ethiopia's lack of support for U.S. opposition to the Soviet presence in Angola proved. And it carries costs, for it associates the United States with regimes or practices that may come to be unpopular. Moreover, unless it has a clear termination date, it tends to create dependence rather than self-reliance on the part of the recipient. And it gives the recipient influence, for it creates a sense of responsibility and commitment which, even though it is emotional rather than legal, may come to tie U.S. hands in a crisis.

Thus the general thrust of U.S. policy should be toward fostering self-determination in the international environment wherever possible. Security assistance should be held to a minimum because it creates dependence, has a tendency to influence the size and character of forces and even encourage a recipient country to go beyond what it can sustain and support with its own resources, and may encourage political polarization, putting pressure on the opponents of U.S. clients to become dependent on the Soviet Union and China, as in the case of North Vietnam, North Korea, and certain Arab states. Thus each decision to undertake or continue security assistance should be made carefully and only where a clearly defined, likely result is in sight and can be weighed against the costs, political as well as physical, and risks.

Alternatives to U.S. security assistance should be looked at: The sale of arms is politically somewhat more neutral. Economic aid is also politically more neutral and may serve security needs, particularly those of governments that are sufficiently well organized and efficient to be able to shift and allocate resources. In addition, former metropoles such as Britain or France, regional organizations or friends, or the United

Nations may have a more direct and politically acceptable claim or responsibility to be the supporter of a troubled country than has the United States.

If a moderate approach is chosen in preference to a disposition to consider every crisis and threat as a test of the United States' world role, there are likely to be individual international inequities that the United States does not take it on itself to rectify. Though this may seem unjust, the fact must be faced that patterns of international relations are shaped at times by crude and even brutal adjustment to local changes before a stable regional and world balance can emerge. Intervention, either with aid or by direct participation, will not necessarily achieve what the United States seeks—the outcome will not necessarily be better; quite likely the United States will become part of the equation of conflict rather than a potential mediator and will run the risk of turning a local conflict into a broader, more ideological contest. A decision to intervene should be made only after cold assessment of the alternatives and the prospects as well as the costs and the risks of U.S. action, and only if it is regarded as the effective thing to do in the interest of the United States and of the client state.

Such calculations must include the economic or military aid that opposing states—particularly in the Middle East and North Korea—receive from Communist governments. This should not be the controlling factor, however; Soviet arms to Egypt, Indonesia, and even Cuba have not removed those states from the community of states with whom the United States can deal. Fundamentally an assessment should be concerned with what a recipient can achieve with aid, over what period, and at what cost in dollars and political consequences to the United States or in protracted hostilities and destruction in the region.

The sharp confrontation over aid to Angola, in late 1975 and early 1976, is illustrative. The dispute centered on matters of procedure and prerogative. Congress asserted its right to know and act on new military assistance activities; the vote to bar use of Department of Defense funds for arms aid to pro-Western factions in Angola represented a sentiment that security assistance should be explicitly authorized and not undertaken under the guise of clandestine operations through unauthorized transfer of funds or use of funds outside established appropriations accounts.

The debate of course dealt extensively also with the merits of U.S. involvement. The substantial supply of arms from the Soviet Union and the presence of Cuban fighting men in great strength were generally excoriated. But there was no agreement on whether that involvement represented a challenge to the United States or a threat to African or Angolan independence which the United States should take it on itself to counter. It was noted that there was no African consensus, and that more African states (including Nigeria, the largest black African state and a major U.S. oil supplier, and the long-standing U.S. client, Ethiopia) backed the faction supported by the Soviet Union and Cuba than opposed it. Substantial Soviet backing, it was recalled, had by no means led to Soviet dominance of Ghana or Algeria or Egypt, so that the lack of alarm in many African states might not necessarily arise only from naiveté. As for the results to be expected from U.S. intervention, it was noted that the scale of U.S. aid would fall far short of matching Soviet supplies. Aside from the unattractiveness of starting on a ladder of probably escalating demands for more funds, the question arose as to which side could more easily up the ante—and whether the result might be, in addition to protracted and widespread hostilities in Angola, the growing dependence of one faction on the Soviets and a growing and entrenched Soviet presence. In addition, the United States ran the risk of being drawn into the conflict on the side of South Africa.

The consequences and risks and costs of intervention, clandestine or open, did not appear to have been carefully thought through and balanced out. Particularly disturbing, less than a year after the end of the Indochina venture, was the rhetoric of great-power rivalry, cold war confrontation, engagement of U.S. prestige. Political initiatives to contain and terminate the conflict, bring pressure on the Russians and Cubans (particularly through Africans), and hasten and facilitate their departure gained prominence only after military aid had been blocked as the foreign policy tool. The political approach should have been emphasized from the outset.

Skepticism or opposition is frequently voiced against foreign aid and security programs; Angola is only a recent case. The test of foreign policy is not its daily popularity, but its soundness and its consequences, how well it proves to serve the country and its interests. But even sound foreign policy will be undercut without understanding and acceptance—and, better, firm support. Congress, moreover, cannot be simply "managed" and consulted about appropriations for foreign aid and security assistance but must in the end be persuaded. And if the members of Congress do not accept and understand and explain to their constituents the case for foreign aid, including security assistance, the case will not be made. There is no natural constituency for security assistance (there is a limited interested one for arms sales as for exports in general). Executive leadership in foreign policy in this field is peculiarly dependent on votes and at least some active support and advocacy in Congress.

Reestablishing a relationship of confidence between the executive and Congress has not been simple. Until the last few years, funds for security assistance were appropriated with surprisingly few strings and a great deal of flexibility as to allocation and disbursement—subject only to reporting (often classified) of what had been done or to informal consultation with a few senior members of Congress. There has been a concerted effort during the past decade to establish accountability, draw more specific congressional guidelines and boundaries, give Congress a more active role in formulating objectives and programs—broadly, an effort to reassert congressional prerogatives comparable to that which led to the War Powers Resolution of 1973.

Foreign aid and security assistance bills offer congressmen and those they represent an opportunity to influence aspects of U.S. foreign policy and overseas activities in which they have an interest. If their interest results in further legislation that is excessively precise and detailed as to goals and programs and directives and prohibitions, this may be the price that must be paid—after the shocks of Vietnam and the transformations of the world economic scene—for continuation of the program. It may be a less flexible tool of diplomacy, but a surer tool of foreign policy in a democracy in a time of accelerated change. Security assistance needs to be exposed to the full light of information and debate. If the parts that cannot stand this light are permitted to wither away, the rest will be the stronger.

One consideration of major importance in a time of budget stringencies is the relative payoff and priorities for dollars devoted to U.S. defense capabilities as opposed to security assistance. Rising personnel and weapons costs have increased defense expenditures. The per-capita cost of supporting soldiers in some allied forces through security assistance, on the other hand, has undoubtedly in the past been less than the cost of maintaining a U.S. fighting man. The measure can be specious, however. It ignores relative capability and, more important, the fact that U.S. forces are under U.S. control, their readiness is known, they can be brought to bear at various places. Most important of all is the basic fact that adequate and evident U.S. military power is a significant factor in the international military balance. For U.S. allies, it is in all cases more weighty than military assistance—none of them can face up to major opposing powers without U.S. support. The U.S. strategic umbrella for Europe and Japan, and U.S. military deployments on or adjacent to the territory of allies weigh far more heavily for their security than any amount of aid. And even for nonaligned countries, the overall balance of power in which the United States is a key factor is crucial to their security. Funds for security assistance are no longer, if they ever were, easily obtained supplements to U.S. defense appropriations; in deciding how much should be requested and appropriated for foreign military aid, the test should be whether the funds are clearly better used for this purpose than for helping maintain adequate, ready, and well-equipped U.S. forces. Some security programs, rationalized in political as well as common defense terms, will be able to stand this test. Others will at best seem of marginal value.

Practically speaking, if military assistance grants are to be phased out, two elements of the security assistance program, which have tended to give it a life of its own, must be adjusted. These are bureaucratic momentum and the broad discretion given not only the President but at times managers within programs. During the past three decades the bureaucratic machinery that moves the program has become firmly established underneath superficial changes at top Washington levels. When the United States was actively concerned with identifying and meeting threats to most parts of the globe, the Joint Chiefs of Staff developed force requirements for scores of countries. Country teams in U.S. embassies, often led by military assistance advisory group officers, have systematically made annual projections of those requirements and the assistance needed to support them. Even though their reports have no formal status, they sustain the illusion and to some degree the fact of a program with an indefinite life span. Staff officers in State and Defense, and to a lesser degree in the Agency for International Development, routinely include provisions for security assistance in the country programs they draw up. The very existence of a separate security assistance program, with its separate budget, engenders calls for annual proposals from embassies and Washington desk officers—and, indirectly, from host countries whose military and other officials see an opportunity to supplement their own resources. Washington policy officials issue guidelines, often restrictive on budgetary or foreign policy grounds, designed to shape and screen out proposals; but the momentum of an entrenched program is strong. Practical incentives of ingratiating embassy civilian and military officials with their hosts, of continuing a program that provides familiar jobs and channels of advancement, and honest attachment to established goals and activities, all keep security assistance programs moving in familiar paths. Unless new guidelines are set in very specific or quantitative terms, they can simply produce changes in the rhetoric of project justification.

Until recently, both the basic assistance legislation and the annual appropriations bills gave the executive branch flexibility and freedom to adjust programs and reallocate funds. The Foreign Assistance Act and the Foreign Military Sales Act provided broad authority and very general guidelines. Appropriations were made for credits for military sales, grants for equipment, and security-supporting assistance rather than for specific countries or projects. Where ceilings were set (on assistance to Latin America or Africa, for example), the President retained authority to exceed them by 10 percent.[3]

Some of the executive flexibility has been removed. The amounts of excess defense articles that can be used to supplement grants and methods of valuation are now prescribed by statute or appropriations language. Funding for assistance to Southeast Asia was gradually brought back into the foreign assistance appropriation, with only Vietnam remaining till the end in the Defense budget. Access to the Defense budget for funding clandestine supplies of arms for Angola was blocked in early 1976.

The concept of flexibility implicit in President Ford's veto in 1976 of the arms export control bill was the ability, in a free world under constant probe and attack, for the President to respond instantly, with the discretion and resources needed, to any threat that might emerge. In a less menacing world, a more deliberate and specific program and authorization are feasible. Instead of a general program, security assistance programs and appropriations for particular countries or regions of specific size and duration could be coordinated with other assistance or cooperative agreements between the United States and the recipients.

Elimination of all flexibility for the President would not be prudent. Though Congress acted quickly at the time of the October 1973 Arab–Israeli clash to provide substantial emergency aid to Israel, the arms and supplies used during hostilities came from Department of Defense stocks

3. Section 610 of the Foreign Assistance Act, 75 Stat. 442.

under authority of section 506 of the Foreign Assistance Act. Crises or threats warranting equally prompt reaction may occur in the future. One way of providing flexibility is through presidential contingency funds; but they are unlikely to be appropriated in sufficient amount to meet serious dangers, at least until confidence between executive and legislative branches in this area has been restored. In any case, section 506 authority to draw on Defense Department stocks within a ceiling is a better device: equipment and supplies will be ready and at times even stationed overseas; the cost of reducing Defense readiness will force careful weighing of the need and urgency for using the emergency clause.

The basic legislation covering military assistance ought to be thoroughly revised. The development assistance sections of the Foreign Assistance Act of 1961 were extensively revised in 1973 and 1974. The 1976 revision of the security assistance portions of the act was not so extensive. General powers, policies, and authorizations are offset by a maze of particular ceilings and limitations. If future authorizations are to be enacted on an ad hoc basis, this structure could be radically simplified. The cold war image of a free world endangered by international communism still underlies the "statement of policy"; not only may security assistance be provided for "legitimate self-defense" and peacekeeping activities, but also for internal security and "civic action" by local military forces. The latter two missions may be quite normal functions of foreign military establishments, but whether the United States should provide assistance for such functions is debatable.

A more radical change in the military assistance program would be to remove it completely from the Foreign Assistance Act and group it with arms sales legislation. In fiscal 1976 for the first time the authorizing legislation for development assistance was separate from that for security assistance; the separation might logically be carried one step further to the basic legislation for development and military assistance (credits and guarantees for foreign military sales, the largest single component, already fall under the Arms Export Control Act). Basic legislation on security assistance could plausibly be embraced in comprehensive arms export legislation.

Such an approach may not be practical, but it merits debate and consideration. If the most important link is that between all forms of foreign assistance—developmental or security—then the Foreign Assistance Act of 1961 with appropriate revision is a reasonable structure. A major share of security assistance currently is supporting assistance, which is economic aid in form (though not developmental in purpose) that is administered by AID. If the controlling common element is perceived to be arms transfers (more precisely, transfers of defense articles and services) whether as aid or trade, then transferring the military equipment and training components of security assistance to arms export control legislation will commend itself.

Whatever is done with basic legislation, it will be important for both the executive branch and Congress to take account of development assistance, security assistance, and arms sales in considering U.S. relations with other countries or any one of the programs. The total impact and cost and benefit of the three must be considered, and the advantages of each weighed. Will it be better to provide economic assistance rather than arms in seeking base rights or encouraging negotiations? Can a country that needs help with its defense afford to purchase arms, on a cash or credit basis, rather than being given military aid? Are legislative restrictions in one sector being quietly offset by increased aid in another?

Moderation in Arms Sales

The U.S. approach to arms sales should be nonpromotional. Sales negotiations should include frank and honest advice on the suitability of various arms to the political and developmental needs and capacities of purchasing states. Many U.S. military and technical experts have a commendable record of pointing to advantages in adaptability, maintenance, training requirements, and initial or lifetime costs of various weapons. Advice of this kind can be of immeasurable help to inexperienced foreign officials who must assess not just initial purchase cost but total economic burden, or military men who must match procurement plans with manpower and logistics. Beyond these tangible factors are the subtler considerations of whether purchase of the most complex and modern equipment might lead to competitive purchases by neighboring states, and perhaps increase their receptiveness to Soviet arms, advisers, and influence. If the U.S. interest is genuinely in stability and security rather than sales, a range of considerations such as these should be discussed quietly with prospective purchasers, and weighed in the decision to sell.

Recently, an increasing readiness to sell the most advanced and sensitive equipment has been evident. Surely the United States should be concerned with maintaining the margin of technical superiority of its own forces, in both quality and quantity. Such exceptional circumstances as the intense struggle for superiority in air and tank warfare around Israel may merit the commitment of the most sophisticated U.S. arms— but the commitment should be to Israel alone and not to its antagonists as well. As a rule the case for selling favored clients the most advanced prestigious gadgets is weak militarily, and the political gain likely to be short-lived, as refusing them to other clients will stir ill will or approving their sale will cheapen the earlier favor. Holding advanced technology for U.S. forces will be understood even if impalatable, and it could have an incidental moderating influence on the international flow of arms.

If U.S. policy is genuinely nonpromotional with a preference for moderation and restraint in arms buildups, this should be made known both to prospective purchasers and other suppliers—not in pious public professions and general disarmament debates, but through senior officials as they meet their counterparts personally. And actions must not contradict words. If military programs and arms acquisitions appear to Americans to be receiving disproportionate emphasis, the practical and prudential reasons for limiting them may be equally compelling for other supplying states and for neighbors of prospective purchasers. There is no reason why U.S. sensitivity to the scale of arms acquisitions should call into question the sovereignty and basic responsibility of other states. The wisdom of arms sales generally or in particular cases ought to be open to question, and the United States should be ready to consult with other states on pressures or problems troubling them and to take concerted action to ease them.

If it intends to foster a more judicious approach to sales, the United States should not seek to be the *exclusive* arms supplier of states in an area. It does not hurt U.S. interests for the British or French to sell to Iran, Saudi Arabia, Kuwait, or the sheikhdoms; quite the contrary. Arms sales can strengthen the interest of other major Western industrial states in the political and developmental problems of the Persian Gulf area, where they can make valuable contributions. From the broader perspective of its alliance with these nations, the United States should be prepared to recognize that the impact of the oil crisis and the problem of offsetting the financial drain of price increases are much greater for the nations of Western Europe than for the United States and that the income from their industrial and developmental work will strengthen overall world trade and financial balances.

Avoiding exclusive relationships in arms sales can contribute directly to U.S. political and security interests. Good, close, mutually beneficial relations between states are far more productive than dominance and dependence. The United States does not want to become committed (legally or emotionally) to other states, or directly responsible for them. To avoid becoming so is not "divesting ourselves of responsibility"; it is the corollary of recognizing that sovereign states are responsible for their own political and security courses. It is the obverse of the principle that the Soviet Union should not dominate an area, nor states become dependent on the Soviet Union. It is a recognition that political influence is small except where the interests of states coincide—as witness how little influence the United States has been able to exert to bring down oil prices.

The basic premise of the United States in its foreign relations is to retain its freedom of action, to remain able to act in the light of its own interests. If the United States can form good cooperative relations with all the states of a region, it will not become unwillingly involved in conflict or confrontation between two states nor so committed to one as to antagonize the other. An exclusive arrangement to supply arms can put the United States in a difficult position, as it has recently in Turkey: continuing to supply arms antagonizes the opponents, internal or external, of the government; cutting off supplies puts the government in a difficult logistic position and lays some responsibility for the consequences on the United States. A multiplicity of suppliers would ease that position considerably. And it would reduce the risk that conflicts between their client states may become proxy confrontations of the United States and the Soviet Union.

Within nations, changes of regime whether peaceful or violent may have political or social overtones. The United States can itself become a political lightning rod if its sale of arms helps a regime to hold on to power; such an association increases the difficulty for the United States of accommodating to political change. In Saudi Arabia, for example, arm's-length transactions with the constabulary, which is responsible not only for internal security but for maintaining the ruling group in power, would be reasonable: advice as to its size and organization, and sales of equipment. But assisting, supervising, conducting protracted organizational, training, and advisory programs—even through the device of a civilian contractor—would raise all the problems of U.S. participation in foreign police training, which is banned by statute.

In general, supply of arms should be given little weight in U.S. political relations with other countries. Admittedly, it is an attractive instrument for political influence. Where the interests of the United States and the purchaser are congruent, arms can serve as a link; where interests diverge, arms sales are an illusory source of influence. Other suppliers are generally available. Even when they are not, however, the U.S. sense of responsibility for the fate of clients (such as Israel, Taiwan, and Turkey) is likely to give those countries a great deal of leverage over the United States.

The United States should be ready to sell arms to countries that are seeking to maintain their self-determination and to avoid political dependence on other suppliers, but arms supplies should not be routinely used as an instrument for political influence or making another country dependent on the United States. Dependence begets responsibility and commands an emotional commitment even where no legal commitment exists (as in past U.S. relationships with Ethiopia and Cambodia). The United States should try to keep its relations on a state-to-state basis and avoid becoming attached to or identified with factions or regimes. It should try also to avoid regional polarization, where U.S. supplies for a client (Iran or Pakistan) are pitted against Soviet supplies for a rival (Iraq or India), both to keep political dividing lines from hardening and to stave off U.S.–Soviet rivalry or confrontation, by proxy or directly.

The United States wants arms of U.S. origin to be used only for legitimate self-defense and other purposes consistent with U.S. interests—not for aggression or aggrandizement, not against other friends of the United States. That concern is particularly relevant to exports to Arab states of the Persian Gulf region, where arms supplied by the United States might fall into the hands of other Arabs to be used against Israel in future conflict, perhaps weighting the balance adversely. Stated U.S. policy and contract provisions specifying the agreed purposes and the U.S. right to suspend deliveries are formal safeguards. Dependence on the United States for spare parts and future deliveries gives such stipulations weight.

But U.S. action in similar cases and the purchaser's calculation of what the United States would do if the restrictions on use or retransfer were violated are more important. Here the signals have been mixed: the executive branch did not act to carry out stated policy when Turkey used U.S. arms in the Cyprus invasion, but Congress suspended deliveries for an extended period and later only partially relaxed the embargo. If restrictions on use and on transfer are to be an effective deterrent, all parties in the U.S. government must reaffirm the agreed policy and demonstrate readiness to apply the policy even at some political cost.

In addition to their dubious effect on regional stability and their questionable political utility, foreign arms sales carry hazards for the U.S. economy. Arms exports, though significant, play a modest role in the U.S. international trade balance, compared either to agricultural exports or to petroleum imports. Directing U.S. exports away from arms and toward nonmilitary investment and sales is certainly more prudent for the American economy over the long term. And if U.S. firms or localities can avoid becoming dependent on arms export business, those interests will not compound the difficulties of making sound national decisions when arms sales come into conflict with human rights, with the desire to avoid involvement in conflict, or with other political interests.

Arms Control and Arms Transfers

In the past the United States had a simplistic and exaggerated respect for what arms and aid could do to solve the security problems of the rest of the world. It is essential now not to make the same error with regard to arms control and peacemaking. There are narrow limits to what the United States can do by example or leadership in the short term to limit arms transfers and thereby resolve regional disputes and bring a stable peace and reduction of military expenditures in the developing world. The United States and other nations can work toward these goals, but they cannot be reached quickly or easily, nor by the United States alone.

Often discussion in congressional hearings on arms sales abruptly ends with the comment that "if we don't sell the arms, someone else will." The question, then, is why suppliers don't get together, particularly to avoid being played off against each other by purchasers in unstable areas or by countries that ought to use their funds and foreign exchange for more useful goods and projects.

Limitations on the conventional arms trade have been suggested from time to time in the United Nations and disarmament organs.[4] They have stirred little interest or support. The most active opposition—even to

4. For a detailed account, see *The International Transfer of Conventional Arms*, A Report to the Congress from the U.S. Arms Control and Disarmament Agency (GPO, 1974), chap. 6 and annex C.

modest proposals for publishing information on transfers—has come from importing countries. They argue that what a country does to acquire arms is crucial to its exercise of national sovereignty and to its security, and that controls over transfers are inherently discriminatory, reserving decisions about key armaments to foreigners and the rights of ownership of certain weapons to a limited group of powers. Efforts by great powers to limit the proliferation of conventional arms are considered oligopolistic and an extension of the thrust of the nuclear nonproliferation treaty with its overtones of political condominium. Countries without indigenous arms industries see themselves at a disadvantage vis-à-vis neighbors or rivals who have arms plants and are less dependent on imports. And the developing nations argue that major arms expenditures are made by the industrial countries, who should set their own house in order by limiting their own military budgets and arms levels.

While in theory suppliers might concert to embargo or limit shipment of arms, in practice this would be very difficult. The major suppliers have rivalries, political or commercial, among themselves; they may have political or ideological ties to purchasing countries. Currently purchasers in the Persian Gulf area have considerable leverage with Western arms suppliers, who need oil imports and have adverse trade and exchange balances. Thus neither worldwide negotiations nor suppliers' agreements to restrain competition offer early promise. Suppliers other than the United States and the Soviet Union also export arms to achieve production efficiencies. To escape this impasse, a more modest approach might be tried and limitation arrangements be worked out on a regional basis.

Regional accords have several attractions: they apply to manageable units, with homogeneity, common interests, sometimes an existing regional organization (like the Organization of American States or the Organization for African Unity). The more formidable problems of scope, complexity, and diversity of size and status and interest encountered in seeking universal agreements may also be avoidable.

While experience provides sobering warning against expecting easy or extensive progress, regional limitations remain the most likely road to success. Such accords might be viewed as unnecessary (in Latin America or Africa, for example, where arms expenditures are low), impossible (because of local bitterness and enmity, as in the Middle East or South Asia), or ineffective (as was true of the 1954 Geneva accords and the work of the International Control Commission, the January 1973

Paris accords relating to Vietnam, and UN resolutions on South Africa and Rhodesia).

Locally generated limitations, although they may be difficult to obtain, are most likely to be acceptable and politically viable, as was the Latin American Nuclear Free Zone under the Treaty of Tlatelolco and the Declaration of Ayacucho, signed at Lima in December 1974 by the states of the Andean Pact. The signatory states[5] committed themselves "to create conditions which permit effective limitations of armaments and put an end to their acquisition for offensive military purposes, in order to dedicate all possible resources to economic and social development." Their declaration may have been only hortatory, but some specific, even if implicit, restraint on weapons imports may have resulted from it: avoidance of acquisition of modern tanks, or of a new generation of sophisticated fighter aircraft, particularly of strike aircraft. While it is not easy to draw a clean line between offensive and defensive weapons, some weapons in particular situations can appear threatening and impel offsetting arms purchases by neighbors; they may be attractive matters for agreements.

Often, in considering arms sales, the United States tries to ascertain whether a sale would appear threatening to a neighbor of the purchaser (who may be another friend of the United States). Better than a unilateral assessment of the effect of proposed arms acquisitions would be a judgment by a regional organization that a sale would not be destabilizing or threatening or the occasion for reciprocal arms purchases by other states of the region. No organization at present is in a position to play such a role; any that attempted to do so would probably be accused of intruding in key national decisions. A procedure of this kind is however implicit in the Declaration of Ayacucho; if it should be used, it would be helpful to responsible suppliers as well as to states of the region.

The most substantial near-term possibility for regional arms limitation, paradoxically, is in the region of greatest tension and even conflict— the Middle East. Limitations would not arise from separate negotiations on arms control but as part of interim or final political settlements of political and military disputes. Deciding on types and numbers and deployment of weapons allowed states of the region, and on supply of arms by outside states, will be no less difficult than formulating the political elements of an accord, and there will be challenges and suspicions and

5. Argentina, Bolivia, Chile, Colombia, Ecuador, Panama, Peru, and Venezuela.

disputes in carrying them out. With the United States, the Soviet Union, France, and Britain—all of whom are arms suppliers and also have Middle East interests—as parties and guarantors of an accord, a viable arrangement might be worked out; an effort must be made to reach agreement.

A less likely region for an arms accord is the Korean peninsula. At present, no negotiations are under way there, and tensions and suspicions are acute. Nevertheless, the interests of four major powers—the United States, the Soviet Union, China, and Japan—intersect in the Korean peninsula and are not basically incompatible. All are likely to be participants if in the future the differences between North and South Korea become the subject of negotiation, practical accommodation, and formal settlement. Provisions regarding arms levels and arms supplies might well be an element in such negotiations and accords.

One additional approach to limitation of conventional arms, and incidentally the traffic in them, is through the revision of the laws of war (the Geneva Convention of August 12, 1949, in particular). For a number of years, under the aegis of the International Red Cross, discussion has been under way on various topics, including indiscriminate methods of warfare and protection of prisoners of war and noncombatants. Use of such conventional weapons as napalm and other incendiary weapons and certain delayed-action or fragmentary weapons can be considered indiscriminate or the cause of unnecessary suffering. Limits on their use might more properly be addressed in a disarmament forum, where difficult technical questions of definition and of proper military missions and means are expected, than in a humanitarian discussion dealing with the large-scale suffering attendant on protracted conflict, from dislocation or starvation as well as from weapons themselves. But human feelings of horror and sympathy motivate this exploration of possibilities for restraint. No government or people can afford to take a negative stance toward such efforts.

Impulses toward limitation of conventional arms and arms transfers will continue to appear on the international scene. Some will reflect concern over the interplay between arms buildups and regional tensions and instabilities, and over the costs of arms acquisition, particularly in developing economies. The United States should advocate that regional balances be at the lowest possible levels and work toward concerted international action on restraint.

There is much that is sound in the current U.S. approach. To enter negotiations on force reductions in Europe against a background of broader political efforts at improved East–West relations in Europe is wise in itself and as an example for arms restraint among Third World nations. Negotiations toward a Middle East settlement clearly offer a useful framework and set of conditions for regional arrangements on arms deployment and acquisition. Given past inter-American relations, the low profile but encouraging posture of the United States regarding the Declaration of Ayacucho is wise. In 1977 the United States took action to limit the flow of arms to South Asia and Africa. But in the Persian Gulf and East Asia, arms sales are still more prominent than movement toward restraint.

Lecturing other states or pressing them to restrain their arms purchases would be a generally counterproductive action for the United States. A clear U.S. public and private posture in favor of moderation in U.S. arms sales is realistic in terms of what military power in itself can do to assure peace and stability. It could have more than marginal influence in diminishing the competitive atmosphere among arms purchasers and arms suppliers and would perhaps stimulate some promising moves toward the effective limitation of the flow of arms.

Applying an Arms Export Policy

For the United States, with its long-standing concern with international security, its leadership in technology and industry generally and in weapons technology in particular, and its prominent position in all forms of international economic and political activity, to seek to stand aloof from the arms trade would be quixotic. More appropriate to the United States is a controlled and discriminating policy that seeks to moderate the arms trade and the U.S. role in it. The policy and its application should be a deliberate part of a broader effort to foster emergence of an international system that is less preoccupied with arms and security than the present system. The ultimate goal of U.S. policy should be to strengthen regional and world peace and stability, but the first test of any action would be its impact on U.S. political and security interests. In general, it would be better to ground agreement or refusal to sell equipment not on what other countries seem to need or what appears to be good for them, but on U.S. interests. Those interests include the wish to reserve advanced or sensitive technology for U.S. forces, and to see that deliveries to modernize U.S. forces are given priority over deliveries to foreign customers; the desire not to become involved or to appear to take sides in disputes or conflicts, particularly between friends or allies of the United States; the policy of not being a party to the acquisition of levels or types of arms by one friend or ally that will appear challenging or destabilizing to another; the desire to avoid identification with a repressive or militarily autocratic regime.

The basic decision to purchase arms is of course in the hands of the buyer. If as a sovereign nation a buyer has the right to make his decision to enter the market, the United States has no less a right to weigh its possible gains or losses and decide whether or not to sell. Frequently there will be no reason for the United States to forgo the commercial advantage of a sale, and undergo the resentment of a rejected buyer; but when there are risks and uncertainties, they should be given considerable weight. The arms supply relationship, particularly if it is a nearly exclusive one, creates ties and dependencies that limit U.S. freedom of action and may make it difficult to avoid political if not more substantial involvement in crises. The United States may want or be impelled to accept these consequences; but it should identify and weigh them before undertaking arms sales, rather than allowing political influence or commercial terms to decide a sale.

The provisions of the Arms Export Control Act and the Foreign Military Sales Act offer sound precedent. They call for a systematic examination of each proposed sale to identify benefits and risks for the United States and for the broader U.S. goals of peace and international stability. Applying their criteria is difficult, however, since most of them are judgmental.

One of the main requirements of a moderate arms sales policy is public control over sales, including the transfer of hardware and services and the licensing of foreign production using U.S. technology or equipment. The government should not consider giving up its control of arms transfers. Nor is there anything to gain by shifting the preponderance of sales from government to commercial terms. Relinquishing the government role in sales would not notably diminish their political impact in sensitive areas of the world, it would make control of exports more not less complex, and it would only increase promotional activities. An aggressive merchandising approach is more natural to private firms than to government; if government officials have been too sales-minded, it is easier to correct that by clear instructions to responsible officials than to rely on a licensing system to make the private activities of dozens of firms conform to public policy goals.

Government and private promotion of arms sales should be carefully monitored and controlled. Offices within the Department of Defense and other government units concerned with sales should have a screening, programming, coordinating, and service function, not a promotional one. The most advanced U.S. technology should be reserved for U.S. forces or close allies engaged in mutual defense efforts.

In particular, if U.S. policy is to be nonpromotional, then government credits for sales should be carefully monitored, and provided only in cases of clear security need or in special circumstances. Credits or guarantees from the U.S. government may be needed when major recipients of assistance are changing to cash purchases. For many developing countries, arms purchases do not attract private financing and the government's credit is poor. Yet the repayment record on U.S. loans for military sales indicates that governments give priority to defense in allocating their resources and foreign exchange. The availability of U.S. government credit can introduce an undesirable weighting into other countries' decisions as to priorities.

Where arms sales are feasible, they are better than military assistance. Sales place the onus and responsibility on the buyer to decide what he needs and can afford to buy and operate. Internal economic and political pressures will come into play and will eventually exercise a form of self-discipline. The relative stability of military budgets and arms acquisitions in much of Europe, Latin America, Asia, and Africa shows how this process can work in a reasonably stable international environment and in the face of competing internal demands on budgets and resources.

If such an approach is to be effective, the United States must avoid biasing the decisions of other governments regarding allocation of funds, resources, and foreign exchange for military purposes. Credits should not be used to promote American exports or win sales from Western European competitors. If other Western suppliers on occasion gain competitive advantage, that should be tolerable if the criterion is that the defense needs of responsible arms purchasers should be met. The large majority of U.S. arms sales does not require government credits, and the U.S. competitive position is good in general. American manufacturers can compete without government financing for the larger part of the market. Further, arms sales proposals should be subjected to rigorous, impartial, and adversary assessment within the executive branch. The review process for military sales proposals might call for a formal dossier, particularly for substantial or sensitive cases such as those to be reported in advance to Congress under section 36 of the Arms Export Control Act.

Congressional Review and Oversight

Security assistance, including the funds for credits and guarantees for foreign military sales, involves appropriations and thus is subject to annual congressional review and action. Before 1974, cash sales of arms were subject only to ex post facto reporting and general legislative guidelines; the Nelson amendment to the Foreign Military Sales Act and 1976 legislation gave Congress a more active role. Congress has an essential interest in U.S. arms sales because they are a major element of U.S. relations and foreign policy in many areas of the world. In the formulation of foreign policy, Congress is constitutionally a full partner. The executive branch has responsibility for the conduct of foreign policy, but arms sales are a classic example of how the execution of policy shapes that policy. Congressional oversight, together with executive responsibility, is thus no less essential than Congress's legislative and treaty-ratifying functions—if formulation of foreign policy is seen as a continuing function concerned with what foreign policy proves to be in practice and in changing circumstances.

The current structure charges the executive branch with management or regulation of sales negotiations and supervision of subsequent operations by private firms. This is a proper executive branch function in general, and particularly so in the case of arms sales. It is difficult to see how Congress could undertake the task of acting on each individual sale of arms efficiently or to any advantage; in many cases, special advocacy of business, labor, ethnic, or other local groups might weigh more heavily than considerations of broad national interest.

The indispensable and powerful function of Congress is that of review and oversight, backed by the lawmaking authority. The problem in monitoring arms sales is not in identifying appropriate standards and criteria but in applying them. Will an arms sale be balancing or destabilizing? Will it contribute to an arms race? Will the recipient be made more able to defend himself or more dependent on the United States for support; what political interest does the United States have in the recipient state or regime? Such questions rarely have black and white answers. The need to report to Congress, with the possibility of having to defend an action and even of having it overturned, helps significantly to get a more balanced and reflective weighing of decisions within the executive branch.

Indeed, in this respect the requirement for advance notification of major sales is effective. Veto by concurrent resolution is an awkward procedure for Congress: thirty days is a short time for legislative action on such matters; the bare facts of a proposed sale are hard to interpret, and these facts may be hard to gather. But the existence of the requirement should strengthen the hand of those in executive agencies who see foreign-policy or other drawbacks in a proposed sale. Their objections will have to be weighed more carefully and will be less easily pushed aside on general foreign policy or security grounds.

Because the element of judgment is so central to arms sales decisions, anything that strengthens the adversary process should contribute to the balance and soundness of decisions. Congressional review and oversight, both by questions and by public hearings, contribute to and reinforce the analytic and debating process within the executive branch.

Not only should the individual sale proposal be judged, but priority must be given when one U.S. policy or objective is in conflict with another. Should Jordan be furnished arms to help maintain a moderate regime in Amman, or should the strengthening of its readiness and ability to become involved in future Arab–Israeli hostilities overrule such sales? Do Turkey's NATO posture and continuation of U.S. base rights in Turkey outweigh the statutory provision that U.S. arms must be used only in accordance with the sales agreement and not in conflicts between U.S. allies or friends?

Congress may be an imperfect instrument for dealing with such choices, and subject to pressure from ethnic, commercial, and other special interest groups. But the executive is no more all-wise nor immune from lobbying and pressure; and Congress does bring issues of principle and priority out into the open to be examined and debated. The process may at times be emotional and disorderly, but it is open and responsible. Arms sales are always an important strand of interstate relations, and at times of tension can become the dominant strain. They should thus not be exempt from the basic democratic process of public accountability. Full consensus is no more likely on arms sales policy than on other complex issues where broad national purposes are difficult to reconcile. But out of the occasional clashes and rejections of executive proposals ought to result adjustment and accommodation of views. In contrast with continuing doubts and mistrust, a feeling that policy is rational and responsible and consistently applied might take hold. Such give and take and accommodation might make it increasingly possible for the executive branch to act without risk of outraged congressional or public repudiation with its unfortunate consequences for the execution of foreign policy.

Arms sales ought to be examined in the context of U.S. foreign and international security policy, with incidental attention to military suitability and short-term political impact. Arms rarely have purely military implications, and they may outlive the immediate impact or benefits of their transfer. A broad approach directs attention to alternative, non-military ways of strengthening U.S. ties and building solid relations. Conversely, confusion about overall policy and the rationale for arms sales programs or decisions makes for the kind of uneasiness that the spate of sales to the Persian Gulf states and the lifting of the Pakistan–India arms embargo raised. Congressional foreign affairs committees could perform a useful oversight function by holding annual hearings for major regions, in which overall foreign and defense policies and programs would be set forth and current and prospective arms sales discussed in relation to them. Such hearings would provide a framework for looking at and, where appropriate, raising questions or taking action on sales cases that later were reported to Congress.

The Larger Objective

In the last analysis, arms transfer programs should be related to U.S. efforts to help build a more peaceful and orderly world. Sometimes arms are the appropriate help, enabling a state to deter or repel attack. Sometimes negotiations or less formal political moves should first be tried. The focus should be settlement of disputes and the prevention, containment, and resolution of conflicts. Cease-fires or settlement agreements are likely to contain provisions about permitted levels and imports and deployments of arms, to which U.S. export policies should be geared. In Africa, Latin America, and South Asia, where disputes are localized and arms sales relatively stable, the United States should take great care to refrain from approving sales that might upset that stability.

A sympathetic and cooperative interest in national or regional trends toward restraint or agreed formal limitations will well serve U.S. purposes. The main thrust of realistic efforts to slow and reverse the arms trade must be solid improvement of international relations. A stable international security environment, settlement of disputes and blunting of ideological or territorial claims, improvement of relations among neighboring states to reduce tension and fear, lessening of the status accruing to military power, direction of energies to development and trade, and raising of standards of living—all of these never-finished tasks of official diplomacy and unofficial intercourse among nations and peoples will reduce pressures and incentives to competitive arming. Formal or informal restraints on the arms trade can be a part of this process, although they are unlikely to outpace it. Regional organizations, as they find a common purpose in cooperation on political or economic problems, may also come to damp down or even concert their members' approaches to arms acquisition; the United States and other major arms suppliers should encourage and be prepared to cooperate with any such ventures in regional restraint. Similarly, they should be prepared to support the partial or full settlement of major outstanding disputes (such as the Arab–Israeli conflict).

If U.S. policy is to become one of restraint and moderation in arms sales, and readiness to explore agreement on limitations on conventional arms levels and trade, this will have to be communicated continuously and quietly to other suppliers and interested states at the highest levels. If U.S. actions stress arms sales and military relations and only arms control officials speak of restraint, U.S. policy and preference will be interpreted by actions taken rather than by what second-level officials say.

But even if the United States pursues its proclaimed course of moderation, this will not markedly reduce the world arms traffic or U.S. arms exports in the short term. The United States cannot quickly affect the basic forces, which are external, even though it is the largest supplier of arms, and a strong international influence as actor and example. A major turn downward in arms acquisitions (from local production or imports) in the world will have to come from an easing of international tension, from giving greater priority to development and human well-being. Arms transfers, though on occasion critical for national survival, can in most cases do little to assure local peace or stability, or to constructively influence relations among states. At worst, they heighten tension, fear, rivalry, and levels of violence. At best, they give confidence for pursuing official and private activities directed toward ameliorating strained relations, working out economic and political problems, reducing hunger and want.

These larger concerns deserve priority in the attention of nations. The United States, with its technical and industrial abilities, its still unsurpassed acceptance as a source of constructive political and economic initiatives, and its basic readiness to accept diversity and self-determination as the premise for stable international cooperation, is particularly well placed to turn attention from the arms trade to more worthy concerns. To follow and hold to this course, though, requires a great deal of political courage.

Index